A CURRICULUM FOR THE MIDDLE SCHOOL YEARS

A CURRICULUM FOR THE MIDDLE SCHOOL YEARS

John H. Lounsbury
Georgia College

Gordon F. Vars
Kent State University

Harper & Row, Publishers

NEW YORK, HAGERSTOWN, SAN FRANCISCO, LONDON

Sponsoring Editor: Wayne E. Schotanus
Project Editor: Renée E. Beach
Designer: Katrine Stevens
Production Supervisor: Will C. Jomarrón/Marion Palen
Compositor: Maryland Linotype Composition Co., Inc.
Printer and Binder: The Murray Printing Company
Art Studio: Vantage Art, Inc.

A CURRICULUM FOR THE MIDDLE SCHOOL YEARS

Library of Congress Cataloging in Publication Data

Lounsbury, John H.
    A curriculum for the middle school years.

    Includes index.
    1.   Middle schools.   2.   Curriculum planning.
I.   Vars, Gordon F., joint author.   II.   Title.
LB1623.L58   373.1'9   77-25248
ISBN 0-06-044126-7

Dedicated to
William Van Til
our mentor

CONTENTS

PREFACE

A major educational phenomenon today is the rise of the middle school. Whether viewed as the latest chapter in the continuing junior high school movement or as an essentially new thrust in American education, there is widespread and significant concern over providing effective educational experiences for youth in the middle school or transitional years. Perhaps no other major educational movement today has engendered as much excitement and positive commitment.

Children and youth learn without either teachers or schools. Schools and teachers exist, however, because they make learning more efficient. By their ability to structure the environment, select the lessons, gather together appropriate materials, and utilize specially prepared personnel, schools make the learning of needed information, skills, and attitudes theoretically possible in a minimum of time and with an assumed degree of certainty.

The curriculum—the instructional program, broadly conceived—is the major means by which an individual school seeks to achieve the established objectives. The focus of this book is on the curriculum that is, or should be, provided for youth in the middle school years, generally ages ten or eleven through thirteen or fourteen. As authors, we set forth a curriculum that, in our judgment, is sound and practical, one that takes into account necessary foundations, and is philosophically valid.

Such a curriculum is attainable. It is not a highly complex program dependent upon sophisticated equipment, special facilities, or rarely found personnel. The school for emerging adolescents does not need to be a complicated place. It ought not to be an "institution," a teaching factory, but rather a center for learning and growing, a place especially designed for young adolescents where they are "at home," among friends and peers, with adults who genuinely care about them, surrounded by an array of materials and facilities to support their growth—social, physical, moral, and emotional, as well as intellectual.

To achieve such a school involves undoing much of current practice rather than adding still another "innovative" program or content package. The answer to educational ills too often has been more— more math, more remedial reading, more specialized personnel, more, more . . . Indeed, it might well be said that we have to teach less in order to teach more.

A middle school is as much people as program; therefore this book opens with a chapter on teachers and those qualities of mind and heart so necessary for developing a sound relationship with young adolescents. The key to an effective middle school lies in the proper melding of program and personality.

This brief volume does not purport to be a major textbook on the whole field of middle school education. It focuses specifically on the curriculum and the teacher. It is built around a particular philosophy of education and a resulting plan of organization which we recommend as especially suitable for the education of young Americans in the middle school years.

The book should be particularly useful to the growing host of teachers and administrators who are now giving serious thought to middle school education as a distinct entity in the educational continuum.*

John H. Lounsbury
Gordon F. Vars

* We apologize for the use of masculine pronouns. But we have used this customary form, by which we certainly mean to indicate both genders, rather than the more awkward he/she construction.

THE TEACHER IN THE MIDDLE SCHOOL

The middle school curriculum proposed in this book calls for a special breed of teacher. Not that they need to be better educated, more intelligent, more experienced, or possess more specialized knowledge. Rather, they need to be special by being secure, open, empathic, positive, and caring individuals who genuinely like middle school students and understand fully the nature of middle school education. If the middle school is to achieve its distinctive goals, if it is to individualize and humanize, if it is to foster positive self-concepts and growth in affective areas, the teacher comes front and center. There is no way to implement the type of program needed in the middle school, save through the person of the teacher. No matter what mechanical marvels are provided, no matter what technological tools are made available, the teacher, unquestionably, is the number one audio visual aid in the classroom.

1

The changing nature of teaching

Teaching is so basic a profession that everyone knows what it is; yet it is so infinitely complex and multidimensional that it is nearly impossible to define adequately. The full nature of teaching is still under debate. A great deal of research has gone into teaching, particularly in the past decade. It is increasingly recognized to be both art and science. It has its mundane dimensions such as housekeeping and bookkeeping. It has its mystical moments when the spark of understanding is suddenly struck. Teaching might be likened to an iceberg —that which is seen is only the lesser part of the entire whole. Classroom performance, the exposed part, gets most of the emphasis; but the unexposed portion is ultimately the more important. The curriculum planning done away from school may have more long-range impact than any one lesson. The brief exchange with an individual student between classes may be the most influential act of the day.

Current recognition of the many facets of teaching makes it clear that the earlier simplistic definitions are both inadequate and invalid. Few today would restrict teaching to the presentation of information. Few would view the job today in terms of the schoolmaster of the past—giving assignments, hearing recitations, and keeping order.

Yet, the traditions of the teacher as schoolmaster and fountain of wisdom are deep-seated. To a nation whose educational institutions have long emphasized the acquisition of knowledge and the maintenance of order, it is difficult to accept the affective domain—attitudes, beliefs, values—as a part of the teacher's responsibility. But only as the middle school comes to deal fully with the broader objectives of education, can it fulfill its mission. The failures of some junior high schools are stark reminders of this need.

When conducted in the institutional setting, teaching seems all the more difficult because of these long-standing assumptions and expectations. The school teacher is beset from the start by gaps between society's expectations of him, his perception of his role, and his students' perception of a teacher's role. By tradition, teachers and students start out at opposite poles, with different, even conflicting, purposes and goals. Resolution of this initial dichotomy requires a change in the expectations of both teachers and students. Most frequently, a compromise evolves which permits activities to proceed, but which is not wholly satisfactory to either party. A new, mutually understood base, growing out of a better understanding of the nature of learning and teaching is needed, so that teachers and pupils may become true partners in the adventure of learning.

Painful and difficult as it may be, middle school teachers today must come to grips with the changes that have occurred in their role. Once the educational broadcaster, the teacher has become more the educational troubleshooter. He can no longer be the prime information source, for modern culture provides many, and often better, media for presenting information.

Despite the acknowledged shortcomings of television, for example, teachers must face the facts about the awesome influence and power of this mass-produced miracle. Elementary age children watch TV an average of 25 hours a week; middle and high school students 15 hours a week. By the time they get to school, children have seen the faces of people all over the globe. Today's high school graduate has spent about 11,000 hours in school—and 15,000 hours watching television! Under these circumstances, the analogy of children as empty mugs to be filled from a teacher's full jug is doubly false. However deficient their skills may be, students most certainly are not without knowledge.

The special importance of middle school teaching

Teaching in the middle school years carries with it a particular responsibility—and an exciting, though awesome, opportunity. This opportunity makes middle school education of special, even crucial, importance. Younger children usually accept with little question the values and beliefs of their parents and teachers. But as young people pass through the middle school years they go through a value system metamorphosis. Early adolescents raise significant questions about right and wrong, God and man, individual values and human relationships. They reject the heretofore accepted answers of others and come up with their own conclusions to questions. Of course, many of the answers are ultimately the same, but now the responses are their own, not just hand-me-downs. Many children are shortchanged in their early years by parents, society, and circumstances. But transescence, the middle school years spanning ages 10 through 14, is a second chance. During these transition years, young people can be helped to build more appropriate, positive values, and to gain a more accurate view of themselves and the world.

This value appraisal and determination becomes still more important when it is recognized that the codes and philosophies, the self-images, that they arrive at during the middle school years are, with few exceptions, the ones that they hold throughout life. Mature adolescents and adults are much less pliable. There is evidence to support the contention that neither high school nor college really changes the basic make up and values of young people. But the middle school years are fundamental in "the making of men and women."

This important educational responsibility is shared by all middle school teachers, not just core, social studies, or interdisciplinary team teachers.

We might go so far as to make these generalizations concerning the primary role of the three major school levels. The primary responsibility of the elementary school is to teach fundamental skills. The major educational objective of the high school is career preparation achieved through increased understanding of the basic areas of knowledge. The basic educational objective of the middle school is neither skills nor knowledge, but simply "becoming." Helping transescents *to be* may be the biggest job for the middle school. The cultivation of individuality and the development of values seem to overshadow the more commonly recognized goals of formal schooling, though all retain importance. Of course, the peer group plays a vital role here, often in conflict with both the home and the school. All the more reason for the school to deal directly with these concerns, rather than relegate them to the status of a byproduct of school experiences which only rarely touch on the things that really matter. Certainly, the teacher's role throughout remains crucial.

The teacher as a person

Central to much of the current consideration of the nature of teaching, particularly at the middle school level, is a growing recognition of the significance of the teacher as a person. The more teaching is understood, the more it is perceived as a humane, personal, and ethical enterprise. It draws upon the whole teacher, emphasizing values, aspirations, and personality. The fully effective teacher is far more than a capable instructor; he is a person engaged in and immersed in living. This is both exciting and frightening—exciting because educational success may not be as dependent upon external factors such as facilities, materials, organizational arrangements and advanced preparation, as has been commonly thought; frightening because the responsibility placed upon the teacher is awesome. Though just humans themselves, teachers hold the transcendent power of example. They are models who teach consciously and unconsciously at all times, for better or worse, simply by what they are. It means that every human reaction or response, even those made non-verbally, may become an act of teaching for some students. It is extremely important to realize that children and youth tend to model themselves on their teachers, parents, and other significant adults.

The importance of the teacher as a person and as an example has frequently been dealt with in literature, perhaps never more pointedly than by Arthur Guiterman in his magnificent poem, "Education," the key lines of which read:

No printed word nor spoken plea
Can teach young hearts what men should be,
Not all the books on all the shelves,
But what the teachers are, themselves.[1]

A teacher's most powerful tool is neither knowledge, wisdom, authority, nor experience; a teacher's most influential tool is his personality. This "self as instrument" concept emphasizes the fact that it is the total person who relates, empathizes, reinforces, and shares feelings. A wink may be more moving than a fact; a touch of the hand of greater influence than a red pencil correction.

Teaching is a very personal art, highly dependent upon human dynamics. The most significant influences of teachers are very subtle in nature and rest largely on the personal relations involved. They are built through the cumulative effect of numerous small actions that occur in daily associations. The learning that makes a difference in living is often the learning that is caught, not taught.

The really important factors in determining success in teaching may be little things—simple, obvious, and human. A teacher may have greater need for sensitivity training than for a course in methods and materials; for a values clarification experience than an advanced course in a subject area. The simple failure to perceive students' inner feelings can negate and void years of scholarly study and achievement in one's chosen field. Indeed, the shortcomings of teachers are almost always ones of attitude and emotion, not ability and achievement. Though such views border on the heretical, they warrant serious consideration by all who would staff a school for emerging adolescents.

Every teacher functions in a self-made atmosphere, a special climate that determines and is determined by his relations with other people. Young people, including those not very good at reading the printed word, have no trouble "reading" this atmosphere. Therefore teachers must be "for real," genuine, authentic. No fake or phony can teach effectively. Teachers must have credibility with students. Sydney Harris has ably expressed the concept of the authentic teacher in these sentences.

A person is either himself or not himself; is either rooted in his existence, or is a fabrication; has either found his humanhood or is still playing with masks and roles and status symbols. Only an authentic person can evoke a good response in the core of the other person. Only person is resonant to person. Knowledge is not enough. Technique is not enough. Mere experience is not enough. This ability is not possessed by those who have failed to come to terms with their own individuated person, no matter what other talents they possess. Until they have liberated themselves (not completely, but mostly) from what is artificial and unauthentic within themselves, they cannot communicate with, or counsel, or control others.[2]

So often the all-important personalized, individualized facet of teaching lies completely outside the realm of teacher-initiated verbalization, the "public teacher." It occurs in fleeting bits of student-teacher interaction that are all but unconscious to both sender and receiver.

Nothing is more fundamental to success in human interaction than the quality of the interpersonal relationships. Teaching and classroom learning, for the most part, occur in the context of human relationships. The extent of learning which results is directly related to the quality of those relationships. The more teachers can demonstrate the qualities needed for good human relationships, the greater will be their effectiveness in meeting the learner's needs. Furthermore, since it is the teacher who largely determines the human relationship climate of the classroom, it follows that whatever should and can be done by teachers to create good human relationships, ought to be done.

Building good human relations in the middle school is complicated by the fact that transescence is a period when young people begin to reject adult influence. In fact, one definition of an adolescent is "a young person who has just become too old to take advice!" Middle school teachers must maintain their integrity in the face of young people who are with them one minute, against them the next; who are often turned off to any adult, no matter how authentic; who resent, as prying, the teacher's efforts to reach out to those who show signs of being troubled. This, then, is the real test of middle school teachers as persons—to maintain their own integrity, to strive continuously for wholesome relations with associates of all ages, and not to take personally the testing, confrontation, and rejection directed at them by transescents as a natural, normal, and indeed necessary part of their growing up.

Developing students' self-concepts[3]

Teachers have always played an important role in assisting youth with developing self-concepts. However, only in relatively recent years, as perceptual psychology has come to the forefront, has this facet of teaching been openly acknowledged as part of the teacher's responsibility. With this recognition has come a certain degree of embarrassment, for it is clear that much of organized education—with its emphasis on competition, its assumption of fixed, inherent ability, and its built-in certainty of failure for some—is diametrically opposed to the new understandings of the self-concept.

One's behavior, in school and out, is primarily and largely determined by what one thinks of oneself, by one's self-concept. It is an abstraction, a gestalt, a conglomerate of perceptions. A person's self-concept is learned behavior. A person learns or develops a self-concept from the feedback of others, from the quality of experiences with people in general. There is, literally, no such thing as a self-made man or woman. Some things, such as learning to ride a bike, are learned from interactions with the physical environment, but most things are learned from interactions with people. Especially important are those whom the psychologists call "significant others"—largely parents and teachers.

This idea existed before perceptual psychology was formulated. Bible verses could be quoted to reflect it. The familiar statement, "Children Learn What They Live," is embossed on posters, plaques, and scrolls in nearly every bookstore in the country. This statement, attributed to Dorothy Law Nolte, says, in part:

> If a child lives with criticism
> He learns to condemn.
> If a child lives with hostility
> He learns to fight.
> If a child lives with ridicule
> He learns to be shy.
> If a child lives with security
> He learns to have faith.
> If a child lives with approval
> He learns to like himself.

The self concept serves as the basis of reality for the student, for it determines what he sees, experiences, and perceives. People tend to "see" that which is congruent with their already existing concept of self. Once affirmed, the self-concept becomes something of a screen or filter through which everything else is heard, evaluated, and understood. There is a circular effect to the self-concept. It tends to maintain itself and to reinforce its existence. In spelling, for instance, the major problem often is the pupil's belief that he cannot spell rather than any inherent lack of ability to spell. Believing he cannot, he does not, and he avoids opportunities to try. The vicious cycle thus perpetuates itself.

But this cycle can work in a positive way too. If the self-concept is learned, it follows that a positive self-concept can be taught. This is a fundamental premise for middle school teachers who seek to guide youth in their quest for identity and maturity. Change comes slowly, but it does occur as conscientious efforts are made to provide success experiences and to reinforce positive actions. People who believe they can, are much more likely to succeed.

Research studies on the effects of a teacher's expectations, such as those in the book, *Pygmalion in the Classroom*, are also pertinent for middle school teachers. How teachers view children, their expectations and attitudes, may significantly alter growth and achievement. Rosenthal and Jacobson state:

> By what she said, by how and when she said it, by her facial expression, posture, and perhaps by her touch, the teacher may have communicated to the children of the experimental group that she expected improved intellectual performance. Such communications together with possible changes in teaching techniques may have helped the child learn by changing his self concept, his expectation of his own behavior and his motivation as well as his cognitive style and skills.[4]

As these views have come into the mainstream of education, they help teachers to realize the need to accentuate the positive rather than harp on the negative. Glasser's concept of "schools without failure"[5] is beginning to have a major impact. Teachers have always been adept at spotting error, at pointing out faults by red pencil, rod, and reprimand. Indeed, this is the stereotype of the teacher in literature and cartoon. Studies of classrooms in action reveal that such a stereotype is well founded, for negative feedback significantly exceeds positive feedback. Providing positive reinforcement has not been considered part of the teacher's job. To reverse that ratio, special in-service programs, books, and even college courses have come into existence.[6]

Closely related to ideas about the self-concept are newer theories about the concept of ability itself. These views are earth shaking for they run counter to many established assumptions that underlie formal schooling. For many years educators assumed that "some had it and some did not." The school's job was to discover and nurture pre-existent and predetermined ability. Ability, it was believed, was largely one dimensional, fixed, and unalterable. Newer discoveries and theories are challenging such views by saying that ability is shifting, variable, and multidimensional. The educator's job, then, is to assist in increasing an individual's capacity to learn. We teach students not just to increase their knowledge, but rather to increase, literally, their ability to learn.

While these views may still be under investigation, the implications for middle school teachers are clear. At this critical juncture in life, when one's adult values and self-concept are being hammered out on the forge of daily experience, the middle school teacher must be fully sensitive to his importance in this process and to his opportunity to contribute positively to the improvement of mankind through helping transescents build better self-concepts. What he believes about children and youth, about ability, makes a major difference.

Middle school teachers might well keep before them that one-sentence sermon of the German philosopher, Goethe, who said: "If you treat an individual as he is, he will stay as he is, but if you treat him as if he were what he ought to be and could be, he will become what he ought to be and could be."

Understanding and utilizing
nonverbal communication

The renewed attention to nonverbal communication in the classroom is another important educational development. While much of what is said and written about this topic is seemingly obvious and conventional, these understandings have too often remained below the level of consciousness for most teachers. Our society, particularly its schools, has been overly enamored of the printed word; yet most of the meanings we derive from others come from nonverbal sources—"beyond words," "silent language," "body language,"—all are phrases commonly used to label this form of communication.

Despite the significant influence of the peer group during transescence, the teacher remains a prime determinant of the nature of the myriad communication "events" that occur in the classroom. He needs to increase his own sensitivity to what is being communicated nonverbally, both by the teacher and by the students; he needs to be able to positively capitalize on the many dimensions of nonverbal communication. We communicate a great deal by our use of time, of space, of color, by our gestures, posture, and touch. We "say" so very much by our facial expression.

Generally, pupils have learned early in the game of school that one expresses personal needs verbally only cautiously and infrequently. They learn to substitute nonverbal ways for expressing their real feelings. Even today, students do not usually say outright, "Teacher, I'm bored to death," but they say it with pencil tapping, slouching, and other "readable" ways. The effectiveness of their communication usually exceeds the readiness and willingness of teachers to receive it.

Whenever there is a discrepancy between verbal and nonverbal messages, people always rely on the nonverbal; dogs and childen even more so. We and they know better than to trust words.

Many nonverbal messages are actually sent and received below the level of conscious awareness, either on the part of the sender or receiver. This is particularly true in the way we employ time, space, and posture. Hence the importance of seeing oneself on videotape, as discussed later. James Thompson's little book, *Beyond Words: Nonverbal Communication in the Classroom*, is an excellent, easily read summary of this field, and is well worth reading.[7]

Tools for self-improvement

Thus far we have stressed the personal qualities demanded of the middle school teacher. Too often these seem beyond the reach of self-improvement efforts. Hence, the necessity of teachers enlisting the aid of colleagues, guidance specialists, curriculum supervisors, and others skilled in the science and art of helping people become more, in Maslow's terms, "self-actualizing." Fortunately, a whole host of techniques have been developed to enable people to be more open with one another, and hence better able to help one another grow in warmth, empathy, and spontaneity.

Mutual helpfulness is built into the self-instruction "modules" developed at the University of Florida as a major tool in the in-service improvement of middle school teachers throughout that state. Teachers are encouraged to form "peer panels" of three to five colleagues for mutual support and criticism. They try to improve both personal qualities and professional skills through study, discussion, role playing, simulation exercises, and observing each other's classroom teaching. Both preassessment and postassessment are built into these "Generic Teaching Modules" to provide some measure of success.[8]

In the Princeton School System of suburban Cincinnati, Ohio, teachers complete self-assessment instruments, identify aspects of their teaching that they wish to improve during the year, and then select "counselors" to help them achieve their goals and evaluate progress. The counselor may be a fellow teacher, a principal, a guidance specialist, or someone from the central office staff. Help from such a self-selected counselor is somehow easier to accept than from someone officially appointed by the powers that be.[9]

Even without the aid of others, teachers can improve through self-examination and reflection. Recently, however, a variety of materials and books have been published to support this technique and to give it more depth. These include both philosophical treatises and activity manuals, including such titles as: *Discovering Your Teaching Self*,[10] *The Teacher You Choose To Be*,[11] and *The Making of a Teacher: A Plan for Professional Self-Development*.[12] These books, and others listed in the references at the end of this chapter, contain numerous activities designed to help teachers improve their interpersonal skills, thereby helping students to grow and develop as human beings.

The development of the videotape recorder has done much towards giving the teacher at least some of the power Robert Burns longed for, to "see ourselves as others see us." Audiotapes have long permitted teachers to hear themselves and their students, but only videotape allows them to monitor their nonverbal communication.

Microteaching, the term often applied to self-analysis of teaching behavior by means of videotaping, has become an accepted feature of many preservice teacher education programs. Less expensive, simpler, and more reliable equipment makes this technique increasingly available to the in-service teacher. The video playback is very revealing, sometimes almost brutal, in its depiction of a teacher's performance. It encourages serious self-examination and develops an awareness which acts as a strong motivating force toward positive change.

Simply seeing one's self in action can be very enlightening; but to apply one of the systems developed for recording and analyzing one's teaching is even more effective. Perhaps the most widely known is "interaction analysis", pioneered by Ned Flanders.[13] These systems provide schemes for observing and coding interchanges among teachers and students, either verbal, nonverbal, or both. The symbols are then tabulated and graphically presented to portray a "picture" of teaching.

Statements may simply be categorized as teacher talk, student talk, silence, or confusion; or a variety of subdivisions may be used to focus on chosen aspects of the teaching process. One teacher may want to examine the kinds of questions being asked, another may wish to analyze the logical dimension of classroom dialogue, whereas another may want to determine positive and negative affect conveyed. There are many different systems, and teachers are encouraged to develop their own to meet their particular needs.[14]

Whichever system is used, data are generated to help the teacher discover the degree of consistency between classroom operation and projected goals. This information helps to answer such questions as: Do I talk too much? Do I encourage student ideas? Do I give praise frequently? Does my "body language" communicate acceptance or rejection?

With videotape or audiotape a teacher can analyze performance in total privacy. It is still more desirable for teachers to work together, observing one another and sharing reactions to both the live and the taped class session.

Most interaction analysis systems do not yield a global score or rating, but they make possible a detailed analysis of the human interchanges that occur in the classroom. Teachers, anxious to understand and improve their teaching, find them excellent tools for self-improvement.

Probably the most important tool for self-improvement is feedback from students. The glint in students' eyes, the way they sit in their seats, and other nonverbal signals communicate to the teacher how a lesson is coming across. Many teachers keep question/suggestion boxes prominent in the classroom and solicit feedback this way. More formal questionnaires may be used from time to time, ranging over everything from the values students see in the subject matter to personal mannerisms of the teacher. Of course, some wisecracks and other irreverent comments can be expected; but most students will respond with as much sincerity as they perceive in the teacher. Openness to students of any age is the mark of an effective teacher, and it is essential at the middle school level.

SUMMARY

Middle schools call for a special kind of teacher—one who is positive, personable, and sensitive to the special dimensions of the job.

The nature of teaching has changed considerably over the years; the media have decreased the teacher's importance as a source of information. This decrease in sole responsibility, however, has been counterbalanced by a substantial increase in new responsibilities in areas of personal growth involving human interaction, personal development, and counseling.

Because emerging adolescents are arriving at their own values and self-concepts, the middle school has a special and enduring importance. The middle school teacher is very much in the ethical business of "making men and women" as well as "schooling children."[15] Supporting and assisting the development of positive self-concepts is a major part of the job of the middle school teacher. It calls for overt and conscious attention with an eye on accentuating the positive.

The changes in emphasis of the teacher's job and the ethical importance of this level, underline the significance of the teacher as a person. Success in middle school teaching depends partly on what you know, and partly on what methods you use; but most of all, it depends on *who* you are. To be effective with transescents, teachers need to be secure and genuine as people, able to utilize fully their personalities as instruments of education.

Since much, if not most, of the meaning people derive from others stems from nonverbal sources, it is important that middle school teachers become sensitive to this recently rediscovered aspect of communication.

Important tools for self-improvement include videotaping, various types of interaction analysis, colleague observation, and direct feedback from students. Self-improvement is a never-ending process for those who aspire to be truly effective middle school teachers.

References

1. Cited in *The Tenth Yearbook* (1950), Future Teachers of America, National Education Association, Washington, D.C., p. 42.
2. Sydney J. Harris, "Authenticity and Teaching," syndicated newspaper column, Field Newspaper Syndicate, Chicago, Illinois, February, 1964.

3. The authors gratefully acknowledge the writings and speeches of Arthur Combs, from which much of this section was derived, directly or indirectly.

4. Robert Rosenthal and Lenore Jacobson, *Pygmalion in the Classroom: Teacher Expectations and Pupils' Intellectual Development,* (New York: Holt, Rinehart, and Winston, 1968), p. 180.

5. William Glasser, *Schools Without Failure,* (New York: Harper and Row, 1969).

6. See, for instance, Jack Canfield and Harold C. Wells, *100 Ways to Enhance Self-Concept in the Classroom,* (Englewood Cliffs, New Jersey: Prentice-Hall), 1976.

7. James Thompson, *Beyond Words: Nonverbal Communication in the Classroom,* (New York: Citation Press, 1973), 207pp.

8. *Florida Modules on Generic Teaching Competencies,* available from Panhandle Area Education Cooperative, P.O. Drawer 190, Chipley, Florida 32428.

9. *Self-Appraisal Instrument, Junior High Edition,* rev. ed., (Cincinnati, Ohio: Princeton City School District), 1973.

10. Richard L. Curwin and Barbara S. Fuhrmann, *Discovering Your Teaching Self: Humanistic Approaches to Effective Teaching,* (Englewood Cliffs, New Jersey: Prentice-Hall, 1975), 223pp.

11. William A. Proefriedt, *The Teacher You Choose To Be,* (New York: Holt, Rinehart, and Winston, 1975), 209pp.

12. Robert M. W. Travers and Jacqueline Dillon, *The Making of a Teacher: À Plan for Professional Self-Development,* (New York: Macmillan, 1975), 114pp.

13. Ned A. Flanders, Analyzing Teaching Behavior, (Reading, Mass.: Addison-Wesley, 1970).

14. See, for example: Anita Simon and E. Gil Boyer, *Mirrors for Behavior,* vols. I and II. (Philadelphia: Research for Better Schools, 1967 and 1970).

15. See the special issue on moral education of the *Phi Delta Kappan,* June, 1975, for a number of thought-provoking articles.

SCHOOLS FOR THE TRANSITIONAL YEARS

Once the junior high school was the proud showpiece of America's educational system, with distinct objectives developed to cure acknowledged ills. Yet, for most of its existence, it has been under fire, confused in purpose, and hampered by a consistent lack of specially trained teachers and appropriate special facilities. The middle school, put forward as a better answer, seems, on careful analysis, little different in theory. And, in practice many middle schools leave much to be desired. Where do we stand today in early adolescent education? Is the junior high school obsolete? Is the middle school better? different? Adequate answers to these and similar questions are not easily formulated.

Educators cannot fully understand the current middle school movement without an understanding of the junior high school movement; for the two are inexorably bound together; and in fact, may really be one. Hence, the chapter begins with the historical development of the junior high and a summary of its growth.[1] This is followed by two sections on the middle school movement. In a final section, the organizational issue and some of its many ramifications are discussed.

The junior high school

The rise of the junior high school

The junior high school story is, overall, a success story very much in keeping with the best of American traditions. At the same time, the institution clearly has exhibited many of the weaknesses often found in American institutions.

The statement that an institution is a product of its times is dramatically illustrated by the case of the junior high school. The story began in 1888 when Harvard President Charles W. Eliot, concerned over the increasing age of college freshmen, raised the question, "Can school programmes [sic] be shortened and enriched?" This was a concern he had previously expressed to his own faculty, and which he voiced now at the important national meeting of school superintendents. And so, the school reorganization or junior high school movement began. The original impetus for reorganization was simply earlier and better college preparation, "the economy of time" argument. The separate junior high school had not yet even been suggested. Considerable interest was soon displayed in the proposed downward extension of secondary education, which consisted in most states at that time of four years—grades nine through twelve.

From 1892 to 1918 several major national committees and commissions studied the idea of reorganization. In general, they supported the proposal to add two years to secondary education at the expense of elementary education. It was charged that the seventh and eighth grades were largely repetitious of earlier grades, primarily a review in preparation for high school. The famous bulletin, *Cardinal Principles of Secondary Education*, contained a clear and strong recommendation for the junior high school.

> We, therefore, recommend a reorganization of the school system whereby the first six years shall be devoted to elementary education designed to meet the needs of pupils approximately 6 to 12 years of age, and the second six years to secondary education designed to meet the needs of pupils approximately 12 to 18 years of age.
>
> The six years to be devoted to secondary education may well be divided into two periods which may be designated as the junior and senior periods.[2]

While a separate junior high school was advocated, the proposed division was intended as part of the secondary level and was neither viewed by this Commission nor by most other earlier advocates of reorganization as an intermediate or middle level.

Even during this initial period some shifting could be noted in the philosophy underlying the various committee reports and discussions. At first reorganization was supported along the lines of Eliot's thinking—teach college preparatory subjects earlier. As more public school educators became involved, reorganization was supported for different reasons—reasons having more to do with the best here-and-now education of early adolescents. The economy of time notion, though the original source of impetus, went by the boards rapidly.

The pioneer research studies of dropouts made between 1907 and 1911 by Leonard P. Ayres, George D. Strayer, and E. L. Thorndike, lent support to reorganization proposals.[3] The statistics reported on the grade repeaters and drop outs were appalling. One third of all the children were retarded in grade placement. One sixth of the pupils in any one grade were repeating that grade. Considerably less than half ever reached the ninth grade. Reorganization was therefore advocated for what it could do to keep students in school longer through a revised and enriched curriculum. It also sought to ensure their regular progress through the grades. "Improved holding power" became the second byword of the reorganization movement. In addition, it was suggested that a new school unit could better provide the vocational training these early school dropouts so desperately needed.

Many thought that one of the major reasons for the high rate of drop outs during the junior high school years was the great gap between the elementary school and the high school. This gulf was caused by sharp differences in philosophy, curriculum, and organization between grade eight, usually part of the "grammar school," and grade nine, the first year of high school. The separate junior high school was proposed as an intermediate step between the two; hence, a third byword of the junior high school movement became the phrase, "bridge the gap."

During this initial decade of the twentieth century, two developments in psychology also made definite contributions to the advancement of the movement. The first was the psychological theory advanced by the influential G. Stanley Hall. According to Hall's recapitulation or "culture-epoch" theory, the age of adolescence was of prime concern. The future of mankind would be determined, in large measure, by the quality of education received at this crucial age. Hall's two volume work on adolescence was the first major treatise on the subject.[4] In his writings he referred to adolescence as "a psychological second birth" and to the adolescent as "a new kind of being." Those who accepted Hall's proposals, and there were many, quickly perceived the merits in a new school unit especially designed for these unique beings who were going through the physical, mental, and emotional revolution that Hall described.

The second development in psychology that furthered the cause of the junior high school was the new focus on individual differences.

Although everyone knew that individuals differed, early schools operated largely on the assumption that people were more or less alike mentally. Many seemed to believe that differences in achievement were more the result of application, motivation, and effort than native ability. But such notions about the uniformity of school children could not stand up when psychologists like Cattell and Thorndike began measuring and testing. The results were surprising, almost startling, for individuals of the same chronological age differed more that suspected. Differences within individuals were likewise extensive.

And nowhere were the individual differences greater than at the seventh, eighth, and ninth grade levels, the junior high school years. It seemed quite sensible, then, to organize a junior high school in order to better work with this diverse adolescent group. The typical self-contained elementary classroom would not permit the grouping or the special experiences deemed necessary to meet these vast individual differences.

These two developments, though contradictory at some points, helped to give the junior high school movement a fourth byword— "meet the needs of early adolescents." This byword has become the movement's theme song and has prevailed even after some of the others have vanished.

Happily for advocates of reorganization, whether they espoused earlier college preparation, more relevant studies for this age, or any other preference, the times in which all of these developments occurred were times of change. Neither national committee reports nor research studies would likely have had much effect, had the culture not been ripe. But these were days of experimentation in politics, home life, religion, economics, and in education. Other contributing factors were immigration, a rising birth rate, and laws relating to child labor and compulsory school attendance. Proposals for reorganization thus fell on fertile soil.

It was the propitious chronological coincidence of these several factors and events, both within and without the realm of education, which made such remarkable growth possible. Though, at some points, the bases which supported the advent of the junior high school were not philosophically compatible, they were concomitant in time, and hence mutually supportive of reorganization. So the new junior high school rapidly became deeply ingrained in America's educational system.

The growth and status of the junior high school

Since the growth of the junior high school movement has been well documented, the full details need not be described here. A limited review and summary, highlighting relationships to the middle school movement, will suffice.

There is no doubt that the junior high school has been phenomenally successful in terms of administrative reorganization. Its advance has been steady, with major growth spurts in the decades following the two world wars. As far back as the 1930s, reorganized secondary schools (those deviating from the four year high school) became the majority practice. By the late 1940s a separate junior high school, followed by a separate senior high school, had become the predominant pattern of school organization in the United States. Table 1 capsules the growth of the separate junior high school. Recent data are not available on the number of junior high schools, but the authors estimate a number in excess of 8000 by the mid-1970s.

TABLE 1[5]   **Number of Separate Junior High Schools**

Year	Number
1916	254
1925	880
1934	1948
1945	2654
1960	4996
1963	7143

Though several states showed a particular commitment to the junior high school, the movement has consistently been a national one with every state reporting some junior high schools by the early 1930s.

Cities have been in the forefront of the reorganization movement because they had the concentration of pupils needed to justify separate schools for different levels. Yet even in rural areas a surprising number of junior high schools have existed. Generally speaking, more pupils than schools were "reorganized", so junior high schools, and their counterpart senior high schools, tend to be relatively large schools.

Although the majority of separate junior high schools have been composed of grades 7–8–9, there have always been substantial numbers of other grade combinations, such as 6–8, 7–8, 7–10, and 8–9 schools. For example, in a 1917 study of 184 junior high schools, Aubrey A. Douglass reported that eleven (6%) of the schools were 6–8 and seventy-seven (41.8%) were 7–8 schools, with a single 5–8 school also noted.[6] Calvin O. Davis' 1918 study of 292 North Central junior high schools included twenty-two (7.5%) 6–8 schools, and one hundred and thirty-three (45.4%) 7–8 schools.[7]

The age distribution of student enrollment and the capacities of available buildings have always been major determinants of school organization. This is especially true at the intermediate level, which may have to accomodate the overflow of students from the elementary school, the high school, or both. Note also the post war spurts in the number of junior high schools as shown in Table 1, attributable in part to the lag in school-building construction during the war years.

Some altering of grade levels and switching of names will no doubt continue, especially as the newer middle school label increases in popularity. Newly organized intermediate institutions will nearly all choose the current label, but the junior high school, defined either by grade level or by school designation, does not yet seem moribund.

The middle school

The emergence of the middle school

The junior high school has never been without its critics, and its demise was predicted more than thirty years ago; however, no specific or major alternative captured public attention until the early 1960s. The term "middle school"—long used in Europe and in some American private schools—was revived, given a particular set of educational attributes, and put forward as something new. It caught hold and soon a full-blown movement was under way.

Samuel Popper has argued that the junior high school is America's middle school,[8] but in current jargon the term usually means an intermediate school without grade nine and beginning with grade five or six. The middle school movement has gained impetus from at least three main sources: (1) the concern for academic excellence and specialization; (2) the belief that young people are maturing earlier; and (3) dissatisfaction with the typical junior high school.

The first source derives from the Sputnik-induced obsession with academic achievement and the mounting pressures for post high school education. This renewed interest in college preparation is a reversion to the college preparation impetus which characterized the junior high school in its infancy.

Many people argue that the needed college preparation can be best achieved in a four year high school, where specialized courses in such areas as science, and necessary sequences as in foreign languages, remain within the fold of the college preparatory institution —the high school. Here too, highly qualified subject specialists can be found. These specialists were needed to handle the "new" mathematics, "new" science, and other restructured content packages brought forth during this period by the discipline-centered national curriculum projects. Likewise, adding the fifth and sixth grades to the intermediate unit brings to those grades the benefit of instruction by specialists in various subject areas, in contrast to the "common branch" or elementary teacher.

Such views and developments have strongly supported a middle school consisting of grades 5–8 or 6–8, with grade nine "returning" to the high school. In many schools, unfortunately, the ninth grade had never really been an integral part of the junior high. Via graduation credits, junior varsity athletic teams, etc., it had remained under the aegis of the senior high school. Basically, it was not a matter of the high school recalling the ninth grade, since it had never been given up.

Further support for the 5–3–4 pattern has come from those who believe that young people are maturing earlier, both physically and socially, than their counterparts did in the 1900s. A Connecticut teacher is purported to have said, "If Booth Tarkington were to write *Seventeen* today, he'd have to call it *Twelve*." A growing body of research evidence points to this earlier maturation. J. M. Tanner, an English scientist, is frequently quoted on his comprehensive studies indicating an earlier age of menarche in girls.[9] Reports of increased height and weight for both boys and girls also are cited to support this view. The degree of correlation between increased physical maturity and mental maturity is not clear but substantial data exist to document the former.

If today's sixth grader is much like yesterday's seventh grader, these educators maintain he requires the specialization of both facility and faculty associated with an intermediate institution. Even those who philosophically disapprove of early sophistication may feel that the handwriting on the wall is clear, whether derived from an improved high-protein diet that induces earlier physical maturation, or by the mass media and social culture that promote precocious sophistication. According to these arguments, school organization patterns may as well reflect this change.

The third major source of strength for the middle school movement is the growing dissatisfaction with the junior high school, particularly with its widely recognized replication of the senior high school in program and practices. This tendency to imitate the senior high school has been evident since the beginning of the reorganization movement. Unable to "free" itself from its big brother, the junior high school readily instituted such practices as interscholastic athletic teams, sophisticated social activities, selection of superlatives (best looking, wittiest, etc.), and other highly competitive activities. It tended also to assume a senior high school posture in teaching procedures and curriculum. A large portion of this criticism, it should be noted, has come from "inside" rather than "outside" the education profession. Over the years, junior high school advocates have been conspicuous among those expressing concern over the failure of the junior high school to be what it was intended to be.[10] At any rate, the middle school was thrust upon the educational scene as the answer to the failure of the junior high school.

In the middle school movement we have seen repeated, with surprising similarity, the multiple causes that characterized the junior high school. Included have been divergent arguments, some actually in conflict, yet all supporting the development of the middle school. Also, like the junior high school, the middle school has been able to capitalize on a series of circumstances unrelated to educational philosophy. The need for additional facilities to relieve overcrowding, consolidation as residential patterns shifted, and the elimination of racial segregation through court-ordered integration plans—all have contributed more to the prodigious growth of the movement than any purported instructional advantages.

The growth of the middle school

The obvious early success of the middle school movement is clear, yet it is difficult to document adequately the growth and current status of the middle school. Fundamental to the problem is an inability to distinguish the middle school from the junior high school, either in grade levels incorporated or in major instructional program characteristics. Many definitions are vague and general and fit junior high schools equally well. Nor is the designation or label of the school a reliable indicator. In the late 1960s relatively few already-existing intermediate institutions adopted the newer label. Some that did so were 7–9 schools whose only change was in name. In the 1970s more of the existing intermediate institutions are converting to middle schools, not only in label but in program.

In the minds of most educators, the junior high school is composed of grades 7, 8, and 9, while the middle school is composed of grades 6, 7, and 8 or 5, 6, 7, and 8. As generalizations, these are acceptable, but they beg many nagging definitional questions. The fifth grade is frequently associated with the middle school; yet its inclusion is widely questioned. A few educators would even include the fourth grade. What is a 6–9 school? Is a 3–8 school an upper elementary school or a middle school? How do you classify the single grade schools all too frequently found at the intermediate level?

Whether the 7–8 intermediate school is counted as a junior high or as a middle school is often a major factor in determining the totals. In some cases these two-year schools were counted in both places, especially in some of the earliest surveys when the middle school was just becoming established.

Many middle schools have been "created" on purely administrative grounds, some almost solely in an attempt to appear "innovative." Brimm has stated it well: "This current period of controversy—middle school versus junior high school—gives schoolmen an excellent opportunity to play the "numbers" game: fitting organization to facilities while pretending to make such decisions on psychological, sociological, and educational principles."[11]

Since the junior high school movement never "standardized" on the 7–9 plan, and administrative factors constantly kept school organization patterns in flux, it is difficult to pinpoint the real beginning of the middle school. The term itself has been used occasionally for over seventy years. In the late 1950s, however, it was evident that dissatisfaction with the typical junior high school was so extensive that realignment and experimentation not based on administrative or school housing factors was becoming essential. A 1959–60 survey of grades 7, 8, and 9 conducted by the United States Office of Education documented this condition. The researchers, Wright and Greer, reported that substantial percentages of the administrators surveyed were planning to alter their 7–8–9 grade arrangement.[12]

The Educational Research Service of the NEA identified 63 middle schools in a 1965 survey of 461 school systems. They defined the "middle school concept of grade organization" as 5–3–4, 4–3–5, or 4–4–4; that is, five years of elementary, three years of middle, and four years of high school, etc. Four years later, in a poll of school systems enrolling more than 12,000 pupils, 235 middle schools were identified.[13]

A survey by Cuff included data on 44 states for the 1965–66 school year. Defining the middle school as one including grades 6 and 7 and not extending below grade 4 or above grade 8, Cuff identified 499 such schools.[14]

The first comprehensive survey was conducted by Alexander in 1967–68. Defining middle schools as "schools having at least three but not more than five grades and including grades 6 and 7," Alexander identified 1101 middle schools.[15] The two year, 7–8, intermediate institution, it should be noted, was not included.

Kealy conducted a comparable survey in 1969–70 using the same definition and identified 2298 middle schools.[16] Only two western states and the District of Columbia reported none. His total represents essentially a doubling in just two years. Over half of the schools (58%) were composed of grades 6–7–8.

In addition, Kealy identified a total of 657 schools that included the term middle school in their names. A few of these included the ninth grade. On the other hand, large numbers of institutions that fit his grade-level definition of middle school were labeled "junior high school," "intermediate school," or "upper elementary school." Some carried no level indication in their designation.

Using the same criteria as Alexander and Kealy, Compton reported a total of 3723 middle schools in 1974.[17] This number represents more than a tripling in the six years since the Alexander survey. Compton also reports the continuing prevalence of the 6–8 pattern, a slight decrease in the percentage of schools with 5–8 and 4–8 patterns, and a slight increase in the 5–7 pattern. Bear in mind that 7–8 schools were not included, though large numbers exist and are often labeled middle schools.

The state by state figures reported by Compton show only the District of Columbia without a middle school. Texas has the most middle schools (407), while California, Illinois, Michigan, New York, and Ohio all have over 200. When grouped by the regional accrediting associations, the North Central and Southern regions clearly had the largest numbers of middle schools.

A more recent survey was conducted by Brooks in 1976. Using the same criteria as in previous comprehensive surveys, he identified 4060 middle schools.[18]

Though difficulties in counting intermediate institutions are apparent, the phenomenal growth in the number of middle schools is evident and unquestioned.

Whether these middle schools represent an improvement over the junior high school is a different matter. It is clear from available research that the middle school, like the junior high school before it, is subject to the same gap between theory and practice that kept the junior high school from reaching its expected potential.[19]

Gatewood, a recognized student of the middle school movement, has summarized the available research in an article entitled, "What Research Says About the Middle School."[20] Citing and summarizing more than a dozen studies, including his own, Gatewood offered a number of conclusions, some of which are quoted here.

> In truth, the only difference between most junior highs and middle schools is in name and grade organization. Founded more upon grounds of administrative expedience than of educational improvement, most middle schools have simply moved the junior high structure, program, and schedule down a grade or two. Or, the programs of grades 5 and/or 6 from the prior elementary school and that of grades 7 and/or 8 from the junior high are maintained so that, in reality, two very different schools are housed in the same building. Most of the research on the topic reports that middle schools tend to have the same high school–type of program of studies, departmental organization, Carnegie units, interscholastic athletics, and early socialization activities that have long characterized and plagued junior highs.
>
> Based upon these findings, it should come as no surprise that several studies have found a significant gap between the main tenets of

the theoretical middle school concept proposed by leading middle school authorities and actual educational practices in most middle schools.[21]

A 1975 study comparing the middle schools and junior high schools in the state of Florida, however, showed several significant differences. The middle schools displayed a number of desirable program characteristics more frequently than the junior highs.[22]

Though not yet convertible to objective data, there seems to be a marked progressive "spirit" among middle school educators. This positive professional concern should result in notable programmatic improvements in the immediate future.

The organizational issue: some points of view and perspectives

When all is said and done—and of course, it never will be—where do we stand on the organizational issue? Unfortunately, extremism has been employed by both advocates and defenders of various positions. In the paragraphs to follow, the authors set forth what they believe to be some logical points of view and some perspectives on the organizational issue. It is hoped that these may help educational leaders resolve organizational problems in their varied local situations.

A separate intermediate institution. The idea of a separate intermediate educational institution has gained wide acceptance among administrators, teachers, parents, and the young people themselves. Common sense, cumulative experience, research, and informed opinion all support the belief that the needs of early adolescents are best met in a school specifically designed for them. Although the idea of housing all twelve grades under one roof in a huge "extended family" has been successfully implemented in a few places, such as the St. Paul Open School, it does not appear feasible in most school situations. Many schools still operate on 7–5, 6–6, or 8–4 patterns; however, in such cases these arrangements are likely to be dictated by building and/or pupil-population factors, rather than being advanced as intrinsically desirable. Moreover, junior high or middle school "divisions," "houses," or "wings" usually exist in buildings that house a wide span of grade levels.

Underlying this acceptance of the concept of intermediate education is the recognition that early adolescence is a distinct stage of development. Between childhood and adolescence is a period of transition during which substantial changes in physical, social, emotional, and intellectual aspects of life occur. Although each individual undergoes these transformations, the specific time and duration of the transition differs widely. A separate institution staffed with adults who are sensitive to these changes and committed to helping young people deal with them can best serve students during these formative years.

Although school organization is not the major issue, there *are* very real instructional and program implications in organizational arrangements. To say "Good teachers make good schools, period!" may have considerable validity, but it is not very realistic. In as extensive an operation as American education, a separation into levels or school units is a virtual necessity on purely administrative and logistical grounds. Once accomplished, each institution is free to create its own atmosphere and identity.

Theoretically, individual seventh grade teachers *could* provide essentially the same instruction, whether the grade happened to be located in an elementary school, a middle school, or a junior-senior high school. But the centrality of the school, its very focus, presents an overriding and ubiquitous influence. Circumstances make it more difficult for seventh grade teachers to meet their young students' needs if they are located in a junior-senior high school, where status is accorded the senior high school athlete, scholar, or student leader. If, on the other hand, seventh grade teachers seek to serve early adolescents in an elementary school, one designed primarily for children, they may find themselves out-of-step with the school atmosphere and environment, its schedule, facilities, and inherent emphases. Inevitably and inexorably the "label" of the school, its public image, and its student body influence, both overtly and unconsciously, the general nature of the program. This is one reason why the new label "middle school," may have much importance.

Organizational arrangement.   Any attempt to justify one intermediate grade grouping over another on the basis of student homogeneity is futile. Some arguments hinge on whether seventh graders resemble sixth graders to a greater extent than eighth graders or whether ninth graders resemble tenth graders more than eighth graders. This overlooks a fundamental concept. An intermediate unit is established not to bring together pupils who are alike, but to bring together pupils who are *not* alike. It is the diversity of early adolescents that call for special programs and a separate institution. Their lack of similarity is what they have in common.

Whatever degree of homogeneity might be achieved by grouping in September would have all but evaporated by February or March; for the changes that occur during a school year are greater than the changes that occur during the summer months. And the degree of homogeneity achieved by any arrangement would be minuscule in comparison to the heterogeneity remaining.

As a rule, a three year intermediate unit is to be preferred over a two year unit. The longer time and developmental span permits greater continuity of teacher-student relationships and course sequences. However, an interesting study conducted years ago in Jefferson County, Colorado, raises some questions about the validity of this common position. The academic achievement, personal-social adjustment, and activity participation of seventh grade pupils in five different organizational patterns were studied. Among the conclusions were the following:

1. Pupils who attended schools with only one or two grades experienced advantages in academic instruction over boys and girls enrolled in schools with three or more grades.
2. When a majority of the pupils in the school were above a particular grade level, the participation of pupils in that lower grade group in school activities was likely to be less than in schools where that particular grade level was not overshadowed.[23]

Although all the pupils are either "coming" or "going" in a two year unit, the increased focus and attention on those two grades may become an asset. Many principals of two year intermediate units are supportive of them and do not seem to long for either the ninth grade or the sixth grade. Here again, it is the educational program offered, not the grade grouping per se, that makes the difference.

Placement of the ninth grade. Whether the ninth grade belongs in the middle school or in the high school is still an unresolved issue. Arguments for returning it to the high school include: greater student maturity, readiness for more advanced instruction and social activities, and an added year in which high school guidance departments can size up students who are bound for college.

Edward Davis examined this issue in his comparative survey of 35 middle schools and 35 junior high schools in New York State. He found that a majority of administrators from both types of schools favored removal of the ninth grade from middle level schools in order to facilitate grouping consistent with student maturity levels.[24]

On the other hand, those who would retain the ninth grade in the intermediate school argue as follows: The bulk of the "transition" to adolescence is accomplished in the seventh and eighth grades (except for some boys). These youngsters now need a year of consolidation and a period of leadership opportunities before being subjected to a new school environment. With the ninth grade retained in the intermediate unit, they have this chance. If moved into a four year high school, these unsure young adolescents become "freshmen," overwhelmed by a more complex operation and unlikely to be given chances at leadership.

Furthermore, it has yet to be proved that placing ninth graders in the high school results in greater academic achievement. A study by Virgil Strickland of 676 ninth graders in two Florida schools resulted in a virtual draw on the question of whether students achieve more success in senior high schools than in junior high schools.[25] And junior high school principals and others surveyed by Gruhn and Douglass tended to support the 7–8–9 organization as the one under which a superior academic program can be developed.[26]

Whether the ninth grade should be in the middle school or the high school depends in large measure on the nature of the high school program and staff. The first year of high school should be designed to meet the special needs of these young adolescent students and to help them make the transition from the middle school. Perhaps a special cadre of ninth grade teachers and counselors is needed to give these students the psychological support that many of them need. In the absence of these conditions, ninth graders are apt to be better off in the middle school.

Placement of fifth and sixth graders. The companion question of whether fifth and sixth graders are better served in a middle school than in an elementary school is also unanswered. For example, a well-designed research study by Glissmeyer failed to show any significant differences in academic achievement over a one year period when he compared 186 sixth graders in partially-departmentalized middle schools with 176 sixth graders in self-contained elementary grades.[27] The results of this California study were in line with other studies that have failed to show an advantage in achievement between pupils in different organizational and grouping arrangements.[28]

Whether supported by research or not, there is, increasing consensus on the practice of including the sixth grade in the intermediate unit.

On the other hand, the placement of fifth graders in a middle school is quite debatable. Gradually, it seems both the advocacy and the practice of including fifth graders in the intermediate unit is slackening. Relatively few nine and ten year olds have reached puberty, and hence would seem out of place in an institution geared to students in transition. The overshadowing effect referred to earlier would also apply with a vengeance to children this immature.

Sensitive to this likelihood, middle schools that include grade five often segregate them somewhat from older students, and provide them with a program similar to the partially self-contained elementary school pattern. As a general rule it might be better to leave the fifth grade in the elementary school and fully integrate sixth graders into the middle school program and activities. A core or home-base program, as discussed in Chapter Five, can provide sixth graders with the security they need while getting accustomed to a new school. As in the case of the ninth grade, the program and staff of the receiving school are the critical factors.

Jurisdictional problems.   When the ninth grade is removed from the intermediate institution, something of a jurisdictional dispute arises in many states. The junior high school has generally been considered "secondary" by state education departments, professional organizations, teacher preparation institutions, and accrediting agencies. Without the ninth grade, however, such an institution may be classified as "elementary." This may change the amount of state aid funds, teacher and administrator certification required, and standards and procedures for accreditation. Such conditions, of course, should not be cause for reorganizing or not reorganizing, but they are realities to be considered and dealt with.

Lack of identity.   Despite the acknowledged growth of intermediate education, however defined or cataloged, it still lacks the identity, recognition, and status that it has long merited. A 1968 study by Pumerantz,[29] which sought to determine state departments' recognition of middle schools, showed that the onset of the middle school had not altered the passive, almost laissez-faire, attitude about intermediate education that has prevailed for decades. Gradually, however, separate intermediate teacher certification is being instituted in several states. A 1975 survey showed considerable, though still inadequate, progress had been made in developing separate middle school teacher certification as compared with a 1968 survey.[30] A National Middle School Association was formed in 1974 and is a thriving professional organization with a quarterly journal, annual conference, and many state and regional affiliates.[31]

The authors' position.   Early advocates of the middle school too often made their case unfairly by attacking the typical junior high school as it exists in practice. To compare the theoretical model of the middle school with the operational junior high school inevitably favors the middle school. Similar differences are found if one compares the same typical junior high school with the long-advocated theoretical model of the junior high school.

   School programs reflect the educational ideas popular at the time they are created. Thus, team teaching, individualized instruction, "open school" plans and the like are found in both middle schools and junior high schools which originated in the late 60s or early 70s. Emmett

Williams refers to this "accident of birth" as a major cause for differences in program between middle schools, most of which are of recent origin, and junior highs, which tend to be older institutions.[32]

The educational rationale of the middle school is essentially equivalent to that of the junior high school. The middle school's primary distinction may be the inclusion of younger children in the intermediate unit. In terms of curriculum, the middle school movement might well be regarded as the renaissance of the "real" junior high school movement. There are far too many improvements to be made in the educational programs provided during the middle school years to waste time and energy fighting a needless internal battle. Phrases such as the "middle school vs. the junior high school," or even "middle school-junior high" with its implied dichotomy, might well be dropped in favor of the "junior high/middle school," the slash mark indicating that these are two names for essentially the same thing.

The authors are neither arbitrary and doctrinaire defenders of the traditional junior high school nor eager champions of the "new" middle school.[33] Both organizational patterns are, at the same time, quite defensible, yet inherently vulnerable. The authors *are* strong believers in intermediate or early adolescent education. Generally, we question the wisdom of placing the fifth grade in the intermediate institution, as recommended by some middle school advocates, but under certain circumstances, this is a very acceptable practice. Similarly, we find a two-year school acceptable, but we feel that a three year school is still more desirable. We believe that the focal point of any intermediate institution, no matter what its label or grade composition, is diversity. Arguments over the purported advantage of one organizational arrangement over another are not intellectually resolvable, and often draw attention away from important matters like curriculum or staffing.

The late John A. Stanavage, in viewing the first flush of middle school successes, stated: "The middle school is threatening to become a fixed feature in the American educational landscape." Fearful that the middle school may not "be able to withstand its own success," Stanavage warned, "The danger is real and present that it now may mummify both its promises and its failings in buildings and bricks and programs and patterns that could tenaciously outlast the essence of the idea itself."[34] His concern, in the light of the history of the junior high school, is well founded.

Nine years earlier Mauritz Johnson, Jr., summed up the organizational issue as follows:

> The decision as to form of organization will have to be made on practical grounds and on the basis of social and administrative viability. Any pattern is satisfactory that gives identity to youths during early

adolescence, includes at least three grades for stability, and brackets those grades in which significant numbers of pupils reach pubescence.[35]

In most situations, Johnson's formula would result in the following grade combinations: 7–9, 6–8, or 6–9. We would also argue that in some circumstances the two year 7–8 school might be acceptable. Yet we must constantly remind ourselves that major educational shortcomings will not and cannot be corrected by organizational rearrangements. Let us not delude ourselves again—changing names or shifting grade levels will no more lead to significant improvement in the late 1970s and 1980s than it did in the 1920s or the 1930s. Educators who are really concerned with improving instructional programs will have to be willing to deal directly with the teaching-learning environment, classroom by classroom, rather than relying on an organizational answer.

Eventually, the school organization issue may be resolved by the elimination of the grade level concept in favor of some kind of continuous progress arrangement from nursery school through grade twelve. Many years ago, Robert H. Anderson proposed a middle school in which the ages or grade levels would ovelap both the elementary school and the high school.[36] Learning experiences equivalent to grades 6 and 7 would be available in both the elementary and the middle school. Student placement would be an individual matter, depending upon a child's physical and psychological maturity. Similar consideration would govern placement in either middle school or high school for work equivalent to grades 8, 9, or 10. To date there is no record of any school system structured along these lines, presumably because of the costs in duplicated facilities and the difficulty in getting a student, his parents, and the staff to agree on a particular student's best placement.

Ultimately students may enter and leave the middle school according to criteria based on maturity and mastery of skills, rather than on chronological age. However, the concept of grades is so deeply entrenched in both the system and the minds of all Americans, that it probably will be with us for some time. Hence, the curriculum model recommended in Chapter Three retains grade level groupings for learnings in which peer interaction is desirable, but nongraded sequences in certain skill areas.

SUMMARY

Over a span of seventy years American education has given specific attention to schools for the transitional years. During these seven decades, much discussion, debate, and experimentation has taken place to determine how emerging adolescents can best be served in the educational enterprise. While both successes and failures have been cataloged, the successes clearly outweigh the failures, and intermediate education has claimed a firm place in the scheme of American education, no matter what grades or labels ultimately become associated with it.

It is an asset to the movement that it is still in flux. But this condition also requires that all who work in these transitional years be aware of the experiments of the past as well as the realities of the present. Only then can the continuing efforts in middle school education be certain to result in real progress. This chapter has sought to provide that understanding of both past and present as a rationale for positive future action.

References

1. The material in these first two sections is derived largely from previous writings of the authors. For documentation and details, see particularly Van Til, William; Vars, Gordon; and Lounsbury, John. *Modern Education for the Junior High School Years,* (Indianapolis: Bobbs-Merrill, 2d ed., 1967), Chapter 1.

2. Commission on the Reorganization of Secondary Education, *Cardinal Principles of Secondary Education,* Bulletin 1918, No. 35 (Washington, D.C.: U.S. Department of the Interior, Bureau of Education, 1918), pp. 12–13.

3. Leonard P. Ayres, *Laggards in Our School.* (New York: Russell Sage Foundation, Survey Associates, Inc., 1909). George D. Strayer, *Age and Grade Census of Schools and Colleges,* Bulletin 1911, no. 5 (Washington: U.S. Dept. of the Interior, Bureau of Education, 1911). E.L. Thorndike, *The Elimination of Pupils from Schools,* Bulletin 1907, no. 4 (Washington: U.S. Dept. of the Interior, Bureau of Education, 1907).

4. G. Stanley Hall, *Adolescence,* vols. I and II (New York: Prentice Hall, 1905).

5. Table derived from data presented in William Van Til, Gordon Vars, and John Lounsbury, *Modern Education for the Junior High School Years,* (Indianapolis: Bobbs-Merrill, 2d ed. 1967), p. 42.

6. Aubrey A. Douglass, *The Junior High School,* Fifteenth Yearbook of the National Society for the Study of Education, Part III (Bloomington, Illinois: 1917), p. 88.

7. Calvin O. Davis, "Junior High School in the North Central Association Territory," *The School Review* (May, 1918), pp. 324–336.

8. Samuel Popper, *The American Middle School: An Organizational Analysis.* (Waltham, Mass.: Blaisdell Publishing Company, 1967.)

9. J. M. Tanner, "Sequence, Tempo, and Individual Variation in Growth and Development of Boys and Girls Aged Twelve to Sixteen," *Twelve to Sixteen: Early Adolescence,* edited by Jerome Kagan and Robert Coles. (New York: W. W. Norton, 1972), pp. 1–24.

10. See, for instance, John H. Lounsbury and Jean V. Marani, *The Junior*

High School We Saw: One Day in the Eighth Grade, (Washington, D.C.: Association of Supervision and Curriculum Development, 1964.)

11. R. P. Brimm, "Middle School or Junior High School? Background and Rationale," *NASSP Bulletin* (March, 1969), pp. 1–7.
12. Grace Wright and Edith Greer. *The Junior High School—A Survey of Grades 7-8-9 in Junior and Junior-Senior High Schools, 1959–1960,* (Washington, D.C.: U.S. Office of Education Bulletin, 1963).
13. Educational Research Service, *Middle Schools in Action,* Circular No. 2, 1969. (Washington, D.C.: American Association of School Administrators and Research Division, N.E.A., 1969), p. 1.
14. William A. Cuff, "Middle Schools on the March," *NASSP Bulletin* (February, 1967), pp. 82–86.
15. William M. Alexander, *A Survey of Organizational Patterns of Reorganized Middle Schools,* U.S. Dept. of Health, Education, and Welfare, Office of Education, Cooperative Research Project 7–D–026, 1968. Summarized in William M. Alexander and others, *The Emergent Middle School,* 2nd ed. (New York: Holt, Rinehart, and Winston, 1969), pp. 161–224.
16. Ronald P. Kealy, "The Middle School, 1960–1970," *The National Elementary Principal* (November, 1971), pp. 20–25.
17. Mary F. Compton, "The Middle School: A Status Report." *Middle School Journal* (June, 1976), pp. 3–5.
18. Data provided by Kenneth Brooks, University of Kentucky, in a letter to the authors dated May 31, 1977.
19. Educational Research Services, *Summary of Research on Middle Schools* (Arlington, Virginia: ERS, 1975).
20. Thomas E. Gatewood, "What Research Says About the Middle School," *Educational Leadership* (December, 1973), pp. 221–224.
21. *Ibid.,* p. 222.
22. Paul George, "Florida's Junior High and Middle Schools," *Middle School Journal* (February, 1977), pp. 10–11, 23.
23. William D. White, "Pupil Progress and Grade Combinations," *NASSP Bulletin* (February, 1967), pp. 87–90.
24. Edward L. Davis, "A Comparative Study of Middle Schools and Junior High Schools in New York State," Ed.D. Dissertation, University of New Mexico, 1970; cited in *Summary of Research on Middle Schools,* pp. 28–29.
25. Virgil Strickland, "Where Does the Ninth Grade Belong?," *NASSP Bulletin* (February, 1967), pp. 74–76.
26. William L. Gruhn, "What Do Principals Believe About Grade Organization?," *Journal of Secondary Education* (April, 1967), pp. 169–174.
27. Carl H. Glissmeyer, "Which School for the Sixth Grader, the Elementary or the Middle School?", *California Journal of Educational Research* (September, 1969), pp. 176–185:
28. *Summary of Research on Middle Schools,* pp. 6–11.
29. Philip Pumerantz, "State Recognition of the Middle School." *NASSP Bulletin* (March, 1969), pp. 14–19.
30. Paul S. George, Marvin McMillan, Robert Malinka, and Philip Pumer-

antz. "Middle School Teacher Certification: A National Survey," *Educational Leadership* (December, 1975), pp. 213–216.

31. National Middle School Association, Box 968, Fairborn, Ohio 45324.
32. Emmett Williams, "What About the Junior High and Middle School?", *NASSP Bulletin* (May, 1968), pp. 126–134.
33. See: John H. Lounsbury and Gordon F. Vars, "The Middle School: Fresh Start or New Delusion?", *National Elementary Principal*, vol. 51, no. 3 (November, 1971), pp. 12–19.
34. John A. Stanavage, "Beyond the Middle School: A Review and a Prospect," *American Secondary Education* (March 1972), p. 5.
35. Mauritz Johnson, "The Magic Numbers of 7–8–9," *NEA Journal* (March, 1963), pp. 50–51.
36. Robert H. Anderson, "The Junior High School," *Architectural Record* (January, 1961), p. 127.

3
CURRICULUM FOUNDATIONS

Effective schooling for any age or grade level must take into account
the learner and how he learns, the contemporary social and cultural
milieu, the way man generates and organizes knowledge, and the
purposes of education which have evolved. In this chapter each of
these foundational areas is examined. Thirteen key characteristics or
needs are identified and translated into guidelines for designing a
curriculum for the middle school years. In Chapter 4 the guidelines are
considered in examining ways to organize the curriculum.

The transescent learner and how he learns

The term "transescent," first used by Eichhorn,[1] applies to the young
person who is approaching or passing through puberty, or who has
but recently experienced this notable event. A dominant characteristic
of today's transescent can be summed up in one word—*precocity*.
Young people today exhibit much of the behavior associated with

adolescence at a younger chronological age than previous generations did. There is even evidence that they reach physical maturity—puberty—at an earlier age. Tanner reports, for example, that the age of first menstruation in the United States decreased steadily from 14-plus at the beginning of this century to a little over 12 and one-half sixty years later, although this trend appears to be leveling off.[2]

Whether social and intellectual maturity is a necessary correlate of this apparent physiological acceleration is another matter. Anthropologists have convincingly claimed that adolescence, as we know it, is primarily a culturally induced phenomenon in Western societies. It may well be that because modern nutrition and high protein diets make young people larger and physically more mature than previous generations were at the same age, they are expected to have the social and intellectual interests of older persons. When young people, in response to these expectations actually do behave in a more sophisticated manner, the self-fulfilling prophecy is indeed fulfilled. Yet adults become "up tight" when twelve-year-olds ask for specific birth control information or thirteen-year-old confirmed smokers demand a place to light up during free time at school!

There is, of course, a critical difference between sophistication and real maturity. Transescents need an opportunity to apply their developing intellectual powers in critically examining the cultural forces, such as the mass media, that are shaping their lives. Whatever the causes or qualifications, precocity is a distinguishing characteristic of many transescents today, a fact that must be considered in designing a curriculum for this age group.

The sophistication of the more visible and outgoing members of the younger generation should not blind us to the fact that there are vast differences both between and within individuals. The *diversity* that characterizes youngsters as they enter the middle school years is compounded by the *rapid changes* that take place during this period. Changes during any one school year are often overlooked by those who argue for a particular grade-level organization for the middle school years. For example, some recommend a middle school of grades 6 through 8 because sixth graders are "more like" seventh graders than they are like fifth graders, and ninth graders are "more like" tenth graders. Even if it were true in September, in a few short weeks all presumptions of homogeneity would have to be abandoned.

The different rates at which boys and girls mature is commonly recognized. It has been truly said that in the middle school we have men, women, and children occupying the same classroom. Marked differences also exist between suburban and rural youth of the same age.

Moreover, each individual grows according to his own timetable, which varies from month to month and is not even the same for all aspects of his development. Witness the boy whose bones have temporarily outgrown the capacity of his muscles to handle them effectively, or the girl who for a brief period is "all nose." A compounding of rapid change and highly variable individual growth patterns gives the intermediate unit the most diverse student body of any school unit. A teacher quite literally faces a different group of children each time he meets a particular class.

Arising in part from these growth and maturation characteristics, and heavily influenced by societal forces, young people have identifiable personal-social needs or developmental tasks. Clearly, *self-understanding* is of primary importance to any young person going through such a period of change. Today's open society thrusts innumerable decisions upon youth without clear and stable societal guidelines. Those concerning sex, smoking, alcohol, and drugs—all of which have far-reaching consequences, both for the individual and for society as a whole—are especially crucial.

In our culture transescence frequently induces a real identity crisis. As the body changes, so does the self-concept. During this process, the individual is extremely vulnerable, somewhat like a recently-molted cricket, his old exoskeleton shed and the new one not yet hardened. These psycho-biological changes are compounded by new expectations from peers, parents, and other adults, generating in many boys and girls the neuroses familiar in the "teenager" stereotype. Fortunately, for most transescents these neuroses are both mild and temporary.[3]

A second major and related need or task is to acquire the knowledge, skills, and attitudes essential for good *human relations*. The adolescent's traditional preoccupation with his peer group is well-known and constantly redocumented. The burgeoning crisis in human relations, evident at all levels of human society, heightens this long-standing concern of early adolescents. Truly, the survival of mankind on this planet depends upon the success with which young and old deal with the ancient problem of human relationships.

Current notions of how learning takes place feature such concepts as discovery, inquiry, and critical thinking. Piaget reminds us that this is an active process, with the learner reaching out and manipulating his environment, not waiting passively to be stimulated. In other words, learning is essentially a *problem solving* process. During transescence the learner becomes capable of the rational, abstract thinking that Piaget labels "formal operations."

This new "cognitive competence" is central to the changes that occur during puberty, according to Kagan.[4] It is a major factor in his search for identity and in his relationships with peers and adults.

Kagan's insightful analysis of early adolescence focuses attention on the transescent as an emerging philosopher, struggling to establish an autonomous belief system amidst a culture that is rent with conflicts and contradictions. A curriculum for transescents must take into account the learner's increasing ability to grapple with complex problems and to "step outside himself" while doing so.

A number of modern learning theorists also have focused attention on the learner's *perception* of the world. They assert that the change in potential behavior that we call learning is primarily a result of the learner's changing perceptions, at least at the higher levels of functioning that are the main concern of the middle school. Hence, effective learning requires direct involvement of the learner in identifying his present perceptions and in evaluating their adequacy. Even psychologists who emphasize conditioning and reinforcement recognize that whether a stimulus provides positive or negative reinforcement depends upon how it is perceived.

In short, as we look at youngsters who are passing through their middle school years, we see young people prominently characterized by *precocity, diversity,* and *rapid change,* with pressing needs for *self-understanding* and *human relations,* whose learning involves changes in *perception* as a result of active and increasingly rational *problem solving.* A curriculum for this age group must take these dominant features into account. Moreover, all who work with this age group must continue to study, not only the research and publications on these topics, but especially the characteristics, needs, and learning styles of the boys and girls in a particular school or classroom.

The social and cultural milieu

Turning to the social and cultural milieu in which young people are maturing, we find a *pluralistic* society undergoing a value crisis so severe that it shakes the very foundations of our government. In the midst of a host of value conflicts, the school is being called upon to develop students with moral courage, commitment, and dedication. A tall order indeed! As Yamamoto puts it:

> It is not easy to be a child in the world today and tomorrow. Evidently, he is under considerable stress, being required to serve many masters at one and the same time. The child is to learn both to "get along with" others and to "get ahead of" others ("bureaucratic" and "entrepreneurial" orientations, respectively). He is to help compensate for all the frustration, anxiety, and humiliation which his father suffers outside in the dehumanized, industrial world, and which his mother experiences in playing the confusing roles of the American female. Liv-

ing in an urban enclave or in suburban homogeneity, he is expected to learn to make social adaptations with little cross-group experience. He is to learn proper sex, vocational, and life roles when these are not clearly defined and where no adequate models are available. He is encouraged to grow, yes, but grow into what kind of world? A world in which no human significance is felt, no humility is left, and no escape is seen from either the desperate population explosion or the threat of thermonuclear annihilation? Why should he grow at all, especially when he is not recognized as a full-share participant in spite of having all his future at stake?[5]

As noted earlier, it is during the middle school years that a young person becomes capable of grappling with these "incompatible propositions," as Kagan describes them. In other words, adolescence is a time when a person ceases to take the world for granted, a fact which represents both challenge and reward for those who work with this age group.

Obvious as it is, the *accelerated* rate of *social change* must be identified as another salient feature of our contemporary world. Its impact is aptly summarized by the title of Alvin Toffler's influential book, *Future Shock*. Social change, a multiplicity of values and the sheer increase in human population guarantee that mankind will have plenty of *social problems* to wrestle with for eons to come: pollution, race relations, population, poverty, energy, changing family patterns, civil rights, world peace, crime, venereal disease, inflation . . . the list seems endless.

A curriculum that takes proper account of social and cultural factors will involve students in examining their *pluralistic* and *changing* society, rent with so many critical *problems*. Transescents must begin to grapple with some of the basic questions of human existence, formulating tentative answers and considering the implications of these answers for their own behavior.

They can do this best under the guidance of educators who are, themselves, serious students of society and dedicated to the continuing search for "the better way." Educators also must be courageous, as many of these ideas are controversial. Impartial examination of topics like population control, sexism, racism, or militarism may provoke individuals or groups who feel that they have *the* answer.

Organized knowledge

Jerome Bruner may be credited with returning organized knowledge to its rightful place as a basic consideration in curriculum design. Almost a decade after publication of his influential book, *Process of*

Education, Bruner softened his position on the primacy of the disciplines in education. He now affirms the importance of student motivation and the need to make education not only sound in scholarship but also relevant to societal concerns.[6] Whether or not one accepts the premise that instruction should reveal the structures of the various disciplines, it is agreed that schools have a responsibility to give students some conception of the *organization* of knowledge.

One basic issue revolves around how early in life a student should be introduced to the formal structure of a discipline *as a discipline.* In the discussion that follows, the position is taken that senior high school and college levels are quite early enough to begin direct orientation to the scholarly disciplines, although this must obviously be based upon concepts, understandings, skills, and values developed in earlier grades.

In the generation of new knowledge, *specialization* has been and continues to be a powerful tool. Some of the basic skills taught during the middle school years contribute directly to the specialized preparation necessary to become a research scientist, a poet, a linguist, or an auto mechanic. Moreover, during the middle school years, youngsters begin to sort out the many interests they have developed during childhood, gradually narrowing the range as they focus on the few that will direct their adult lives. The school has a responsibility to help in this process. Yet, educators must not encourage students to specialize too early or too narrowly. Scholars from many disciplines decry the narrow vision that may result from carrying this to an extreme. Marshall McLuhan puts it this way:

> Specialization won't work any more as a means of learning. The only technique today for obtaining depth is by interrelating knowledge, whether it be in physics or anthropology or anything else. When a man attempts to study anything, he crosses the boundaries of that field almost as soon as he begins to look into it.[7]

Today's world requires both scholars and ordinary citizens who can generalize intelligently when the occasion demands and who try to see life in its totality. The well-documented *knowledge explosion,* brought about to a large extent by highly-refined specialization, also demands the kind of person who can discover the broad principle lurking behind the mountain of detail. Moreover, the proliferation of knowledge intensifies man's need for improved "information-consumption skills," to use Luvern Cunningham's communicative phrase.[8] Such abilities do not come as automatic by-products of the mastery of knowledge. They must be taught, and such teaching calls for continuous action and innumerable examples.

To give mankind's knowledge its proper place in the curriculum calls for a staff that views the *knowledge explosion* as a challenge to search for and teach fundamental ideas, not an excuse for packing more information into the curriculum. They would temper *specialization* of instruction with a continued attention to the "broad picture," and they would consider the nature and needs of the learner in introducing the more formal *organization* of knowledge. It goes without saying that middle school educators should continue to develop their own scholarly competencies, both as specialists and as broadly-educated human beings.

Table 1 summarizes the key concepts identified above.

TABLE 1   Curriculum Foundations: Salient Characteristics and Needs

The Learner	*Society*
Characteristics	
Precocity	Pluralistic
Diversity	Accelerating change
Rapid change	Social problems
Needs	*Knowledge*
Self-understanding	Organization
Human relations	Specialization
Learning Process	Explosion
Problem solving	
Perception	

Implications for the curriculum

Cursory as it may be, the preceding analysis has identified a number of key ideas that should guide the design of curriculum for the middle school years. Needed is a program that gives adequate *and balanced* attention to the learner, to society, and to organized knowledge. Few would argue with this seemingly obvious and valid generalization, yet it is a sad fact that faddism in education too often leads schools to overemphasize first one foundation, then another.

Curricular guidelines for the middle school years

In a deliberate attempt to keep all of the key concepts which evolved from an examination of the foundations in focus, we propose the following curricular guidelines for the middle school years:

1. *Every student should have access to at least one adult who knows and cares for him personally, and who is responsible for helping him to deal with the problems of growing up.* We have seen how crucial the needs for self-understanding and human relations are during transescence, especially in a perplexing society like ours. Helping students with personal problems is one of the responsibilities of a school guidance program, but few schools can claim substantial success in this area.

2. *Every student should have the opportunity to deal directly with the problems, both personal and social, that surround him.* All pertinent sources of knowledge should be tapped, but it should not be necessary for the student to "detour" through a formal study of the disciplines as they are organized by scholars for the purpose of promoting further scholarship. Problem solving as a *process* of learning should augment the use of problems as a *focus* for content, a most powerful combination, in our judgment.

3. *Every student should have the opportunity to progress at his own rate through a continuous, nongraded sequence of learning experiences in those areas of the curriculum that have a genuine sequential organization.* These provisions are essential to provide for individual differences among learners, including their variable rates of change, and to permit those who are interested and capable to move into advanced work in an area of specialization, like mathematics or foreign languages. This does *not* necessarily mean that the student must be working alone in a carrel most of the school day, however. Indeed, we believe that students can progress successfully through a highly individualized continuous progress sequence only if they have some kind of stable, home base group of their social-emotional peers to provide the necessary security and social interaction.

4. *Every student should have access to a rich variety of exploratory experiences, both required and elective.* Planned experiences in art, music, industrial arts, and home economics ordinarily are required of middle school students. This is a means of acquainting them with some areas of knowledge they might otherwise not encounter in any organized fashion. Electives and student activities are justified as meeting individual differences and providing interested students with further learnings in areas of special interest or ability. Electives are one way for educators to introduce new knowledge or learning activities, to try them out before making them a part of the required program. All of these experiences help the student to learn more about himself, his interests, and his abilities.

Many additional guidelines can be derived from an analysis of the learner, society, and organized knowledge, but these appear to be the most significant for the middle school curriculum.

Purposes of education

In designing curriculum for the middle school years, it is not sufficient merely to examine the foundational areas and derive guidelines. The purposes of education must also be considered.

No matter how elaborate they may be, most statements of the purposes of education boil down to two basic goals: (1) to prepare citizens who can function effectively in a democratic society, and (2) to help each person become a fully functioning individual. Since these are the educational goals of the entire society, many institutions share responsibility for their attainment—the home, the school, the church, the mass media, and voluntary youth agencies. A perennial problem in American education—beyond the scope of this book—is the question of where the school's role ends and that of other agencies begins.

Whatever the school's domain of responsibility, its simultaneous concern for both the good of society and the good of the individual results in curricula composed of both "common learnings" and "specialized education." The common learnings are those that are considered essential for any citizen, regardless of his occupation or station in life. These fundamental concepts, skills, and values bind a society together, making communication and cooperative action possible. Examples include knowledge of our government and its functioning, skill in reading, and respect for the worth and dignity of the individual.[9] Definitive statements of the behavioral goals of general education in both elementary schools and high schools may be found in two volumes published in the 1950s by the Russell Sage Foundation.[10] A staff formulating objectives for today's education would gain a great deal from examining these works. Not only are many of the objectives still valid today, but also the framework of analysis used in these texts provides an excellent tool for grappling with a very complex task.

Specialized education is that which is designed to promote the uniqueness of each individual. Most types of individualized instruction, independent study, elective courses, and student activities serve this purpose. Of course, individual uniqueness may be and often is promoted within common learnings, as when a teacher permits each student to prepare a biographical report on an historical person of his choice.

Since, in the final analysis, each person learns in his own unique way, some "innovative" schools have gone overboard in catering to individual needs, nearly ignoring the need for common learnings. A sound curriculum gives balanced attention to both common learnings and specialized education for individual uniqueness.

SUMMARY

In this chapter we have examined the foundations of the curriculum: the learner and his learning processes, the social and cultural milieu, and organized knowledge. From these we have identified thirteen key characteristics or needs that must be taken into account in designing the curriculum. These in turn were translated into a set of guidelines. Finally, the purposes of American education were examined. In Chapter 4 we consider ways of organizing the curriculum to fit these guidelines and at the same time to achieve the major purposes of education.

References

1. Donald H. Eichhorn, *The Middle School*, (New York: Center for Applied Research in Education, 1966), p. 3.
2. J. M. Tanner, "Growing Up," *Scientific American*, vol. 229, no. 3 (September, 1973), pp. 42–43.
3. Emmett Williams, "Transescence and Identity Crisis," *Transescence*, vol. III (1975), pp. 13–17.
4. Jerome Kagan, "A Conception of Early Adolescence," *Twelve to Sixteen: Early Adolescence*, ed. by Jerome Kagan and Robert Coles. (New York: W. W. Norton, 1972), pp. 90–105.
5. Kaoru Yamamoto, "America in Which Our Children Will Live: An Educational Perspective." Paper presented at the 11th Annual Fall Conference of the College of Education, University of Toledo, Toledo, Ohio, November 11, 1967, pp. 16–17.
6. Jerome S. Bruner, "The Process of Education Revisited," *Phi Delta Kappan*, vol. 53, no. 1 (September, 1971), pp. 18–21.
7. Marshall McLuhan, "From Instruction to Discovery," *Media and Methods*, vol. 3 (October, 1966), p. 8.
8. Luvern Cunningham, "Top Priorities for the Principal: Improving Curriculum and Instruction," Address presented at the 1967 Fall Conference of the Ohio Association of Secondary School Principals, Columbus, Ohio, (October 22, 1967).
9. Gordon F. Vars, ed. *Common Learnings: Core and Interdisciplinary Team Approaches*, (Scranton, Pennsylvania: Intext Educational Publishers, 1969), p. v.
10. Will French and Associates, *Behavioral Goals of General Education in High School*, (New York: Russell Sage Foundation, 1975); Nolan C. Kearney, *Elementary School Objectives*, (New York: Russell Sage Foundation, 1953).

4
CURRICULUM ORGANIZATION

After studying the foundations fully and deliberately, and considering anew the purposes of education, one inevitably turns to the matter of curriculum organization—that general plan which attempts to co-ordinate time, personnel, materials, and content to achieve the objectives of education in a particular situation.

The combinations are almost limitless, although tradition and common practice, together with financial and physical limitations, have established basic parameters. In this chapter we set forth a curriculum organization design which we believe is best for the middle school years. It promotes the goals of American education, balances common learnings and specialized education, and adheres to the guidelines derived from the foundation areas. The chapter also contains three alternate ways of organizing the middle school curriculum as proposed by recognized educators, together with some analysis and comparison.

A recommended curriculum organization

Figure 1 illustrates schematically the overall curriculum design that we recommend. It consists of three main components which are briefly described here and further elaborated upon in later chapters.

The components differ primarily in curriculum structure or organization, not in purpose. For example, common learnings are provided through core, through required studies such as mathematics from within the continuous progress component, and through courses and activities in the variable component that are required of all students. Likewise, specialized education may be provided through optional learning activities within the core component, through con-

Figure 1   A Middle School Curriculum Design

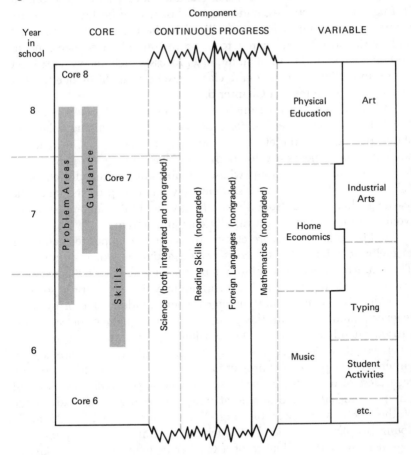

tinuous progress electives such as foreign languages, and through optional courses and activities within the variable component.

Core

A major portion of the common learnings should be provided through a core program, most simply described as a problem-centered block-time program.[1] At its best, core provides students with a direct and continuing opportunity to examine in depth both personal and social problems that have meaning to them. It also provides a situation in which a teacher can know a limited number of students well enough to offer the advisement or counseling most of them need so badly during the transition years, and in the process they can learn essential human relations and communication skills.

Much, but not all, of the content and skills traditionally taught in English, social studies, and science classes may be taught in core, where they become tools to be utilized in the process of inquiry. Art and music, so often relegated to a peripheral role, also become important sources and tools in an inquiry process which knows no subject matter limitations. Whether core classes are best taught by one teacher or a team is examined in Chapter 5.

Grade or age level designations are retained in the core program. We feel that there are definite advantages in maintaining relatively stable peer groups for at least a portion of each day. The teacher-student rapport necessary for both individual and group guidance is hard to establish in a group whose membership continually changes. Likewise, committee work, student government projects, and the learning that results from the daily give-and-take among students would also be reduced in a rapidly changing group.

On the other hand, core classes are scheduled opposite each other to facilitate inter-class and cross-graded activities when appropriate. These are represented in Figure 1 by the dotted line "balloons." For example, certain problems of growing up may be of concern to some of the older sixth graders and younger seventh graders. One of the core teachers could work with this group while the remainder of each class carried on other activities. On occasion, students from two or three levels could work together on a large problem area, perhaps an environmental improvement project to which youngsters could contribute, regardless of maturity or year in school. Short-term skills development groups would also be desirable at times, especially to take advantage of the potential of peer tutoring. Yet, for most activities, 25 to 30 young people would spend as much as one-third of the day working together under the guidance of a teacher or team that is well known to them.

Continuous progress

A second major component of the curriculum should be a set of continuous nongraded learning experiences for those skills and concepts that have a genuine sequential organization. A nongraded or continuous progress curriculum allows for individual differences and variable rates of growth in students, and is responsive to the demands for specialization of knowledge. Science, reading, mathematics, and foreign languages are labeled continuous progress in Figure 1, with broken lines at the ends of each column to indicate that the sequence hopefully extends from kindergarten through grade 12. Nongraded sequences may be provided in both common learnings, such as reading and mathematics, and also in specialized, elective areas, such as foreign languages.

However, instruction in any subject area would not be exclusively nongraded. Science, for example, would be part of the core as it related to such problems as pollution or drug abuse; yet, certain laboratory aspects of the field might readily be taught in a nongraded sequence. The dotted line between science and core in Figure 1 symbolizes this dual nature. Reading and mathematics skills would be taught directly in nongraded programs, but applied and practiced throughout the school program. It is generally recognized that all middle school teachers have a responsibility to further the development of basic skills. Many reading and related fundamental skills are, in fact, best taught in the context of a subject area. Likewise, in many student activities the need to develop skills, such as effective oral communication, is evident and should be met.

Variable

The third major component, labeled "variable", is illustrated in Figure 1 with loosely defined blocks of various sizes and shapes. Many of the activities and programs that have proven their worth in schools are neither so highly sequential as to be placed exclusively in the nongraded component nor so essentially problem-centered as to fit entirely within the core. Art and music, for example, contribute to core in many ways, and they embrace performance skills that could be placed in a nongraded sequence. Yet, who is to say that learning to play an instrument or examining a painting as social commentary represent the whole of the arts? Some argue that the humanities have a logic all their own and that there should be a place in the curriculum for specialists in these areas to develop courses, activities, independent study, and other learning experiences in ways that seem most appropriate to both teachers and students.

One way that home economics and industrial arts may be approached is through student groups which are divided, like the core classes, primarily on the basis of age or social-emotional maturity. Physical education, on the other hand, might better be taught in groups formed on the basis of physical maturity or skill, while grouping in the student activities program would best be determined by interest.

Learning programs of such diversity clearly call for flexibility in grouping, scheduling, and curriculum organization. Moreover, some experiences in this component will be required of all students, and others will be elective. The decisions made here, as in the middle school's overall curriculum design, should be based on an analysis of learner characteristics, societal demands, and the nature of knowledge as applied to each field or activity. Calling this component of the curriculum "variable" is not to suggest that the other components are *in*variable; but that a more uniform structure or pattern characterizes the curriculum design in both the core and the continuous progress components.

This component is not to be considered less important than the other two. We reject the notion that the fine arts or student activities are frills that can be dropped whenever finances are tight. Experiences in these areas may be the most meaningful of all for many middle school students.

Alternative curriculum organizations

There are several other well-known middle school curriculum models that merit the attention of educators. Three such proposals are summarized here, with some analysis and comparison.

Theodore C. Moss proposes a middle school curriculum divided into four areas, as illustrated in Figure 2.[2] The skills would be developed primarily through individual means, especially programmed instruction, although they would be applied and practiced in the academic classes of Area II. Freed of much of the responsibility for skill building, teachers of these academic subjects could emphasize concepts and understandings, according to Moss.[3] Modular scheduling is advocated to de-emphasize the notion that all subjects must meet five times a week and for the same number of minutes each period.

English and social studies are to be taught in a heterogeneously grouped core program, while mathematics and science are taught separately and tracked by ability. All students would study a foreign language for a least one year. Special classes for those gifted in art, music, and dramatics would be provided; both boys and girls would

Figure 2   Middle School Curriculum Design of Theodore C. Moss

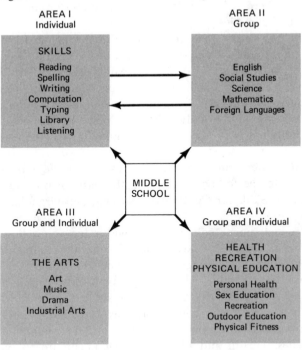

Source: Theodore C. Moss, *Middle School*, (Boston: Houghton Mifflin, 1969), p. 45.

take industrial arts. Home economics is omitted from the program, except on a "part-time basis," presumably because ready-to-wear clothing and "instant meals" eliminate the need to teach cooking and sewing. Health education is taught by a team, and students are grouped on the basis of physical development for intramurals, physical fitness, and gymnastics. Student activities would take place either during the lunch period or outside of school hours, unless they were an outgrowth of classroom activities, in which case they would be included within the allotted class time.

We concur with Moss on the value of a core program for guidance and problem-centered learning. There are some parallels between Moss' individualized skill development area and the nongraded program we recommend, at least for reading and mathematics. However, we question whether spelling, writing, library, and listening skills should be separated so sharply from other classroom instruction. In our judgment, these might better be taught functionally within core or other classes.

We are mindful of the social side effects of tracking, and prefer the plan Moss suggests as an alternate—the nongraded approach.

When all students are moving through a learning sequence at their own individual rates, there is less likelihood that any one group will be stigmatized as the "dummies."

We also feel that there is a definite place in the curriculum for a modern homemaking program, which offers a great deal more than just cooking and sewing. Such programs deal with many aspects of living that are both relevant and vital, such as interpersonal relations, child care, money management, and the like. And we would give student activities a definite place in the daily schedule. Many of the major objectives of the middle school are best met through well planned student activities.

William M. Alexander and associates propose a middle school curriculum divided into the following areas on the basis of purpose: Personal Development, Skills for Continued Learning, and Organized Knowledge.[4]

The personal development component provides for counseling, for the development of values, for health and physical development, and for exploration of interests. Students are assigned to "home-base" groups led by a teacher-counselor, who provides both individual and group guidance and serves as referral agent for students who need more specialized help. The home base group has a regular period, usually daily, for group activities, conferences, and for the examination of values-laden issues. Health and physical development are to be promoted either through a separate course or through a coordinated program involving science, physical education, and home-base teachers. Student activities and both short and long-term electives are to be the vehicles for developing individual interests.

Skills for continued learning are to be developed in every classroom, with specialized instruction for those who need it. This instruction may be provided through special laboratories or study-skills centers, programmed or "automated" instruction, or tutoring by older students. Independent study is also recommended as a means of developing both the skills and the attitudes essential for lifelong learning.

Alexander and his colleagues describe several different ways of organizing the curriculum in the major subject fields of English, mathematics, social studies, and sciences. The following approaches are recommended: (1) Understanding of basic concepts should derive from the student's own investigations, (2) Concepts and skills should be applied to everyday activities and problems, (3) Interrelationships of peoples and cultures should be stressed, (4) Major generalizations from various fields should be used to better understand people and their ways of living, (5) The role of literature and the arts in communication and culture should be explored, and (6) Thinking and problem-solving skills should be mastered.

Furthermore, Alexander and his colleagues propose specific criteria to ensure that balance, continuity, flexibility, and individualization characterize the total curriculum.

The home-base program in the Alexander model reflects a commendable concern for counseling and the study of value- related issues. However, unlike core, such a program may be divorced from the major instructional program. If so, it inherits many of the weaknesses of the conventional homeroom program. Homeroom activities not directly related to the rest of the school's curriculum, and consequently carrying no academic credit and receiving no grades, are too often viewed by both students and teachers as trivial and unimportant.

Moreover, there may be insufficient time in the home base group for the study in depth needed to undergird the examination of current issues. If home-base teachers also teach the major academic subjects, these two aspects of the program may be coordinated around issues or problems. Unless it goes beyond mere correlation, however, such a program cannot match the full-scale study of students' personal and social problems that is possible when home base and academic study functions are combined. in a core program.

Alexander and associates do not propose any specific curriculum design for the teaching of "organized knowledge." They cite examples of block-time and humanities programs, but they are primarily concerned that students learn the "basic concepts in the various disciplines." Such an emphasis runs counter to the wide-ranging study of broad problems that is so central to the core component in the model we recommend. In most other respects, the Alexander model fits our guidelines quite well and reflects a balanced concern for both common learnings and specialized education.

The three components in *Donald Eichhorn's* model (Figure 3) bear labels very similar to Alexander's, but there are differences in the way each is structured internally. For example, Eichhorn's *Knowledge* component is an integrated, interdisciplinary study of man's past accomplishments, present challenges, and future aspirations. Thematic units in this area also draw upon the humanities, arts, and sciences, and emphasize student interests.

In the *Learning Processes* component, students develop communication skills, analytical skills, and technical skills. Analytical skills relate to logical thought processes, such as gathering, analyzing, synthesizing, and evaluating data. Technical skills are those usually associated with the fields of industrial education, art, music, homemaking, and typing. Skill learning is essentially self-paced.[5]

Figure 3   Middle School Curriculum Design of Donald H. Eichhorn

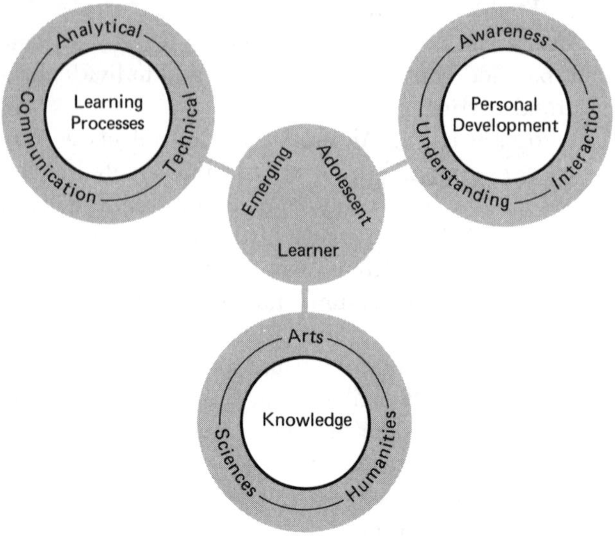

Analytical

Learning
Processes

Communication

Technical

Emerging Adolescent

Learner

Awareness

Personal
Development

Understanding

Interaction

Arts

Knowledge

Sciences

Humanities

Source: Donald H. Eichhorn, "The Emerging Adolescent School of the Future—Now," *The School of the Future—Now,* ed. J. Galen Saylor, (Washington, D.C.: Association for Supervision and Curriculum Development, 1972), p. 41.

In a different source,[6] Eichhorn explains that the component labeled *Personal Development* (or Personal Dynamics) is designed to help youngsters to understand their physical, social, and emotional development through the study of such units as: "Understanding Yourself," "Home and Family Living," "Facing and Solving Everyday Problems," "Ethical Standards and Values," "Growing into Manhood or Womanhood," "Drugs and Alcohol, and Tobacco."

The Eichhorn model, like the others cited, is solidly based on the nature and needs of transescents. Self-pacing in the learning of skills parallels our emphasis on continuous progress; the integrated studies proposed under the rubric of Knowledge bear many of the earmarks of core. The units suggested for the Personal Development component bear a still greater resemblance to core. Eichhorn emphasizes the inter-relationships among all aspects of the curriculum, but we prefer to deal with both the personal and the broader societal aspects of problems in a core program, rather than in two separate components. We agree with Eichhorn's statement that each student must have direct access to a adult who is intimately aware of this youngster in all aspects of his life.

A prototype schedule

The master schedule is an important tool for implementing a curriculum design. In scheduling, an administrator juggles time, staff, students, and school facilities to come as close as possible to the ideal he has in mind. Figure 4 presents a prototype schedule developed for the Opportunity Park Middle School in Akron, Ohio.

The school is made up of two multiage houses of approximately 250 students each, with three interdisciplinary academic teams, an instructional leader, and a counselor in each house. A four-member arts team serves both houses. Each academic team is responsible for instruction in language arts, social studies, science/health, and guidance. In addition, each team member teaches either mathematics or reading during the period when the entire house is regrouped for criterion-based instruction in these two subject areas. All staff members share responsibilities during the school-wide activities.[7]

While no master schedule can guarantee the kinds of learning experiences provided in the classroom, it is apparent that the Opportunity Park Middle School schedule would facilitate the curriculum design proposed in this book.

SUMMARY

Our consideration of the purposes and the foundations of education leads us to propose a three-part curriculum for the middle school years. A core program would provide those common learnings best acquired through a problem-centered approach. Skills and concepts best learned through carefully sequenced learning experiences would be taught mainly in a nongraded or *continuous progress* component. Other worthwhile learnings that are neither primarily problem focused nor highly sequential would be provided through flexibly arranged courses, activities and independent study in what we are calling the *variable* component.

The curriculum designs proposed by Moss, Eichhorn and Alexander and associates provide alternative designs that meet our proposed guidelines to varying degrees.

A carefully designed master schedule, like that developed for the Opportunity Park Middle School in Akron, Ohio, is an important vehicle for implementing a sound middle school curriculum.

References

1. See Gordon F. Vars, "Core Curriculum," and "Block-Time Programs," *Handbook on Contemporary Education*, ed. Steven E. Goodman (New York: R. R. Bowker, 1976), pp. 379–388.

Opportunity Park Middle School Prototype Schedule

Owen House

Grade	Number Students	Number Classroom Teachers	A.M.		P.M.		Activities School-wide
				Reading & Math Skills Block		Academic Block	
6	110	4	Academic Block	All 250 students of house regrouped for criterion based instruction. 1/2 time math 1/2 time reading. Under direction of reading and math specialists, academic block teachers, and auxiliary personnel.	Lunch	Arts/Phy. Ed.	Intramurals Performing Groups Clubs Guidance Activities Projects Special Interests
7	60	2	Arts/Phy. Ed.		Academic Block / Lunch	Academic Block	
8	80	3	Arts/Phy. Ed.		Academic Block	Lunch / Academic Block	

Tenney House

Grade	Number Students	Number Classroom Teachers	A.M.		P.M.		
			Reading & Math Skills Block				
6	60	2	All 250 students of house regrouped for criterion based instruction. 1/2 time math 1/2 time reading. Under direction of reading and math specialists, academic block teachers, and auxiliary personnel.	Arts/Phy. Ed.	Lunch	Academic Block	Arts/Phy. Ed.
7	110	4		Academic Block	Lunch	Academic Block	Academic Block
8	80	3		Arts/Phy. Ed.	Academic Block	Lunch / Academic Block	

Source: Opportunity Park Middle School Educational Specifications, (Akron, Ohio: Akron Public Schools, 1976), p. 48.

2. Theodore C. Moss, *Middle School*, (Boston: Houghton Mifflin, 1969), p. 45.
3. *Ibid*, p. 66.
4. William M. Alexander, et al., *The Emergent Middle School*, 2d ed. (New York: Holt, Rinehart, and Winston, 1969).
5. Donald H. Eichhorn, "The Emerging Adolescent School of the Future—Now," *The School of the Future—Now*, ed. J. Galen Saylor. (Washington, D.C.: Association for Supervision and Curriculum Development, 1972), pp. 35–52.
6. Donald H. Eichhorn, "A Successful Curriculum Change," *Midwest Middle School Journal*, vol. 3, no. 3 (June, 1972), pp. 27–32.
7. *Opportunity Park Middle School Educational Specifications*. (Akron, Ohio: Akron Public Schools, 1976), pp. 43–49.

5 THE CORE COMPONENT

The term *core* sometimes is applied to any type of interdisciplinary program, but it is more properly restricted to block-time programs with a distinctive curriculum emphasis.[1] Specifically, core is a form of curriculum organization, usually operating within an extended block of time in the daily schedule, in which learning experiences are focused directly on problems of significance to students. Conventional subject matter is brought in only as needed to deal with these problems, and core teachers are charged with providing a major portion of the guidance and counseling needed by students.

As in other block-time programs, a core class may be taught by one teacher or by a team; it may occupy from one-fourth to one-half a student's schedule; and it usually replaces English, social studies, homeroom, and sometimes science. The balance of the school program consists of other subjects, both required and elective, and student activities. Any or all of these may be correlated with the activities of the core class.

A core program can benefit students of any age, but we believe it is especially appropriate for the middle school years because it fits the following guidelines proposed in Chapter 3.

1. Every student should have access to at least one adult who knows and cares for him personally, and who is responsible for helping him deal with the problems of growing up.
2. Every student should have the opportunity to deal directly with the problems, both personal and social, that surround him.

Of course, *all* teachers should stand ready to help students with their personal and social problems, and the essence of motivation in any course is to deal with problems and issues that students accept as relevant. However, what is everybody's business too often becomes nobody's business; so it is desirable to have a program in which these two aspects of education are the main foci. In other phases of the curriculum teachers give higher priority to other goals, such as individualization of instruction, as discussed in Chapter 6, or exploration, as discussed in Chapter 7.

Background

Core is recognized by many curriculum experts as one of the few genuinely different approaches to education that have appeared within this century. Although its roots have been traced far back into educational theory, it was a distinct feature of the secondary education programs that evolved during the era of progressive education. In its emphasis on student needs, rational inquiry, and democratic processes, core parallels the elementary school innovations of this period, such as the "activity movement," the "project method," or the "experience curriculum."[2]

Such unconventional programs have always had limited popularity. They constituted approximately 12 percent of the junior high block-time programs identified through surveys carried out in the late 1950s[3] and mid 1960s.[4] The stress on academic learning that followed Russia's space challenge temporarily diverted attention from the core idea, but current efforts to "humanize" and "personalize" education may be viewed as a revival of the core "philosophy." Indeed, many of the so-called "compassionate critics" of education appear to be reinventing the core curriculum under such labels as "humanistic education," "open education," "free form education," and even "career education."

Rationale of core

The rationale of core was recently elaborated by a task force of the National Association for Core Curriculum. Ten basic assumptions and beliefs were identified, with specific implications for both the core program and the core teacher. No doubt many teachers share these assumptions and beliefs; but if they teach in conventional programs, they may find their implementation restricted by schedule, instructional materials, curriculum directives, and the like. Although the complete NACC position paper is well worth reading in its entirety, space permits us to cite only a few selected items.

Assumption I.   Interests, Concerns, and Needs Expressed by Pupils Provide a Valid Basis for Curriculum Content and are Central to the Learning Process.

>   THEREFORE:
>
>   Core makes extensive use of problems of personal and social concern or topics of current interest which have been identified by pupils, rather than content predetermined by teachers.

IMPLICATIONS:

A. The core program provides:
1. Opportunities for pupils to express ideas and concerns.
2. Opportunities for pupils to select, or share in selecting, some of the problems and topics to be studied individually or in groups.
3. For several topics or subtopics to be studied at the same time by different small groups or individuals within a class.

B. The core teacher:
1. Encourages pupils to express their ideas and concerns about problems and topics they want to study through the use of such techniques as: surveys, discussions, small group consensus sessions, etc.
2. Helps pupils to develop criteria for selecting topics for study and to apply the criteria during the selection process.
3. Organizes the class so that individuals and small groups may be working on different topics at the same time.
4. Relates the near-at-hand and easy-to-understand—local issues, school problems, student council, class problems and incidents—to issues of broader concern.
5. Keeps continuous records of observations of pupils, which serve as leads to interests, concerns, and needs.

Assumption II.   Learning Involves Changes in Behavior Which Are Brought about Through Experience.

>   THEREFORE:

A. Core draws on many disciplines and a wide range of informational sources, materials, and activities relevant to the vital problems and topics of personal and social concern.

B. Core provides experiences in sharing information, respecting the rights and contributions of others, and taking responsibility.

.

.

.

Assumption III.   A Democratic Society Values the Worth and Dignity of the Individual.

THEREFORE:

A. Core seeks the optimum development of each individual and his special aptitudes.
B. Core requires that the teacher treat each pupil with humaneness and respect. In turn, the student becomes aware of his own humanity and of his relationships and responsibilities to other human beings.

.

.

.

Assumption IV.   A Democratic Society Requires Citizens Who are Skilled in the Decision-making Process.

THEREFORE:

A. Core emphasizes the development of problemsolving techniques and procedures
B. Core requires that students become actively involved in all class activities.

.

.

.

Assumption V.   Higher Priority Must Be Given to the Development of Learning Skills and the Clarification of Values, Than to the Acquisition of Specific Information in Subject-matter Areas.

THEREFORE:

A. Core includes as its main goals those qualities, competencies, and characteristics needed to become effective and responsible citizens.
B. Core seeks to develop the self-directed learner who will think of education as a continuous lifelong process.

.

.

.

Assumption VI.   Learning Experiences Are Enhanced When the Learner Is Encouraged and Helped to Draw upon All Appropriate Sources of Information.

THEREFORE:

Core helps the student to correlate and integrate his learning.
.
.
.

Assumption VII. The Extent and Nature of Classroom Activity Should Determine the Allocation of Time.
    THEREFORE:

Core is scheduled in extended blocks of time.
.
.
.

Assumption VIII. The Teacher's Primary Roles Should Be Those of An Advisor, A Facilitator, A Friend, and A Fellow Learner.
    THEREFORE:

The core teacher functions as an advisor, a friend, facilitator, organizer, co-planner and fellow learner who assists youth in discovering and clarifying what is important for them to learn.
.
.
.

Assumption IX. Teaching and Many Aspects of Guidance Are Complementary Functions of the Teacher.
    THEREFORE:
        Individual and group guidance are integral elements of core teaching.

IMPLICATIONS:

A. The core program provides:
   1. Evaluation procedures that report more than subject matter achievement.
   2. A flexible curriculum and an extended time block which allow for guidance activities.
   3. Guidance materials appropriate to the classroom.
   4. Opportunities for pupils to examine their problems, values, and concerns.
B. The core teacher:
   1. Regards each student as an unique individual.
   2. Makes an effort to become acquainted with the student's experiences, both inside and outside the classroom.

3. Is constantly attentive to the positive development of the student's self-concept.
4. Provides opportunities for discussions involving value clarification and personal problem solving.
5. Utilizes current literature and techniques concerning guidance.
6. Realizes that student progress should not be evaluated on the basis of academic achievement alone, but also on his ability to accept himself and deal with his surroundings.
7. Recognizes that everything he does has guidance implications.

Assumption X.   To Bring about Continuous Improvement in Learning, All Concerned Parties Should Be Involved in Evaluation.

THEREFORE:
Core benefits from continuous evaluation by teachers, pupils, administrators, parents, and visiting teams.[5]

Two types of core

A core curriculum may be classified either as *structured* or *unstructured*, depending upon the limits of planning set in advance by the staff.

In a *structured* core program, the staff decides in advance which broad problem areas or centers of experience the students will explore. These categories of human experience range from those which are primarily of immediate and direct personal concern to adolescents, such as "Personality Development" or "Sex," to broader social problems like "Pollution," "Population," or "Human Rights." Some of these problem areas may be required at a particular grade level; others may be optional. Within a chosen area, students and teachers cooperatively plan learning units focused on the specific problems and concerns of members of a particular class. The teacher-student planning process has been amply described in the literature, most thoroughly in books by Zapf[6] and by Parrish and Waskin.[7]

Lists of recommended problem areas have been proposed by curriculum specialists from time to time. A most recent example is the following list, derived by Van Til from an analysis of curriculum foundations using a process similar to that illustrated in Chapter 3.

CENTERS OF EXPERIENCE PROPOSED BY WILLIAM VAN TIL:

1. War, Peace, and International Relations
2. Overpopulation, Pollution, and Energy
3. Economic Options and Problems
4. Governmental Processes

5. Consumer Problems
6. Intercultural Relations
7. World Views
8. Recreation and Leisure
9. The Arts and Aesthetics
10. Self-Understanding and Personal Development
11. Family, Peer Group, and School
12. Health
13. Community Living
14. Vocations
15. Communication
16. Alternative Futures[8]

Centers of experience are ordinarily elaborated in a set of resource units, describing the ramifications of the problem area, possible learning activities for students, pertinent instructional materials, and the like. The teacher and students select from these the learning experiences they consider most promising. Selection is facilitated in schools that have access to computer-based resource units, which list learning activities and materials specifically fitted to the characteristics and objectives of each individual student.[9]

In an *unstructured core* program, teacher and students are free to examine any problem they consider worthwhile. For example, here are topics and problems identified by one eighth grade class when asked to list what they considered worth studying. The student committee which organized the list placed some topics under several headings, illustrating how many problems interrelate. Trivial items are minimized when students perceive that the teacher is sincere and that they will be expected to make a serious study of the topics chosen.

SUGGESTED TOPICS FOR STUDY—8TH GRADE,
KENT STATE UNIVERSITY SCHOOL

1. School and campus
   a. dress codes
   b. religion
   c. grading systems
   d. campus unrest
   e. K.S.U. killings
   f. race problems
2. Drugs
3. Population
   a. birth control
   b. abortion
4. Environment
   a. pollution
   b. conservation
   c. poverty (slums)
5. Fashions
6. Crime
   a. shoplifting
   b. rape; sex crimes
   c. hijacking
   d. drugs
   e. riots
   f. police brutality
   g. prison conditions

7. Civil rights
   a. women's lib
   b. race problems
8. Exploration
   a. deep sea diving
   b. space travel
9. Transportation
   a. cars (new developments)
   b. planes
   c. space travel
10. People
    a. generation gap
    b. race problems
11. Young people's demands
    a. ratings on movies
    b. voting age
12. War

a. atom bomb
b. Southeast Asia
c. the draft
13. Health
    a. smoking
    b. venereal disease
    c. drugs
    d. mercy death
14. Beliefs
    a. the occult (E.S.P.,
       witchcraft)
    b. respect for country
15. Economy
    a. prices
    b. inflation
    c. depression

Criteria to guide selection may be established by the staff or by each teacher and his students. These serve to eliminate topics that students have already studied, those which interest only a few, or those for which there are insufficient learning resources. Units developed in unstructured core classes may fall within the centers of experience listed earlier, or encompass several of them. For example, a class may begin studying boy-girl relations, become concerned with the problem of venereal disease, and end up spearheading a drive for wholesome recreation for young people in the community.

Varied roles of the core teacher

In addition to guiding students' investigations of meaningful personal and social problems, the core teacher has other important tasks. Skills must be taught as needed to process the information dealt with in a problem-centered unit. These range from conventional basics, such as reading, writing, and spelling, to more contemporary tools such as interviewing skills, analysis of films, and the techniques of producing a television program. Students explore literature of all types, art, music, and any other expression of civilization's accumulated experience, as resources for studying problems. In addition, core classes may take time to discuss current affairs and to enjoy reading and creative writing experiences unrelated to the unit under study. Since core classes usually serve as homerooms, they carry out the usual school government duties, class recreational activities, and the like.

The core teacher also is a key member of the school's guidance team. Guidance in a core class is offered through curriculum, methods, and personal counseling by a teacher who knows the student well. Core classes study many of the issues and problems ordinarily examined through group guidance. Small group work enables students to share their concerns; just knowing that other students are experiencing the same problems is often reassuring for young people. Moreover, individual conferences between teacher and student are natural outgrowths of such core units as "Growing Up," "Understanding My Sexuality," "Teenage Problems," "Planning My Career," or "Finding Values by Which to Live." In addition to airing student concerns, such units give students an opportunity to judge the teacher. They can determine, by the way he or she reacts to certain controversial topics such as drugs or sex, whether a teacher is sufficiently free of hangups to be open to student discussions of personal problems.

The goal is to ensure that all transescents have access to an adult who will listen without judging as they wrestle with the thoughts, feelings, and interpersonal relationships that accompany growing up. The teacher must demonstrate that he can be trusted with student confidence, and also studiously avoid giving advice, thereby assuming responsibility for the child's problem. Instead, the teacher must encourage the student to examine his feelings, clarify his values, and consider the consequences of a variety of alternatives.

All teachers who undertake such guidance functions must keep in close touch with the professional guidance staff. Without revealing student confidences, the teacher may obtain useful background information about a student and some suggestions as to next steps in helping him. At times the problem may extend beyond the teacher's expertise, in which case the task is to help the student accept referral to a specialist, such as the guidance counselor or the school psychologist. In addition, the guidance department should coordinate the guidance efforts of all school staff members. Active and concerned teachers, backed by an effective student personnel services staff, can make a significant impact on the happiness and well-being of young people going through a difficult stage in life.[10]

Strengths and limitations

In addition to the guidance advantages described above, core has added strengths that stem from the large block of time in which it functions. This makes it easier to use techniques such as teacher-student planning, small group work, creative writing, field trips, and role playing, all of which may be cramped when confined to a single 40 or 50 minute period. Teachers and students become better acquainted, which enhances the teacher's function as advisor or guide. The teacher may assume somewhat the "mother hen" role of the elementary teacher in a self-contained classroom. This is especially important to students who are going through the stresses and strains of puberty. It is also valuable as they move into an unfamiliar situation, such as the transition from elementary to middle school or middle school to high school. The popularity of block-time and core programs in the early grades of junior high or middle schools may in part be explained by the desire to ease students' transition from a self-contained or "open classroom" environment to a more or less departmentalized program.

All interdisciplinary programs that combine or replace two or more subjects facilitate the correlation or fusion of content and enhance opportunities to teach skills functionally in a number of different contexts. Interdisciplinary approaches uncover gaps and duplications between courses, and may lead to more efficient use of time.

The problem focus in core takes it beyond the mere correlation or fusion of content. Student motivation for learning is heightened by the use of problems significant to young people in general; through teacher-student planning and small group work the learning experiences are brought even closer to the lives of a particular group. In the process, students learn vital problem-solving and decision-making strategies through actual practice.

Probably the major reason why the core curriculum is not more widespread is the shortage of qualified teachers. In addition to having a broad academic background, a core teacher must be committed to the kind of philosophy represented by the NACC position paper cited earlier. That is, there must be recognition that the teacher's role is primarily guiding students in their own self-directed inquiry, rather than merely purveying subject matter. Few colleges offer professional programs specifically for core teachers. Prospective teachers are reluctant to prepare for a kind of program that is not widespread, yet school administrators say they cannot initiate or expand core programs without trained teachers—the proverbial vicious cycle. Although colleges could do much more than they are doing at present, it is apparent that schools wishing to develop core programs must rely heavily on in-service education of available staff.

Research on the core curriculum is hampered by the difficulty of measuring such intangibles as a student's self-concept, critical thinking ability, personal and social adjustment, or "democratic" attitudes.[11] Wayne Jennings' study also underlined the difficulty of finding enough genuine core classes, even in a large school system, to compare with the more conventional block-time programs.[12] Too often, studies do not distinguish between types of block-time programs, and many comparisons were made before research techniques were developed to detect subtle differences in such factors as teacher-student inter-action. Yet one thing is evident from the more than fifty-five studies of block-time programs completed to date: students in these inter-disciplinary programs acquire the knowledge and skills measured by conventional achievement tests as well as, or better than, those in separate subject programs.[13]

The National Association for Core Curriculum is now at work on evaluation instruments for assessing the degree to which school programs, teacher performance, and administrative practices reflect the philosophy set forth in the task force statement.

Some admonitions

As with any major curriculum innovation, the development of a core curriculum should not be undertaken lightly. Questions such as the following must be considered carefully:

1. What subjects should the core replace? In the model proposed in Chapter 4, the core class replaces English, social studies, and some aspects of science. This combination is the one most often found in block-time and core programs, but staff members may want to try different arrangements. In the final analysis, it is the content of the program that is important, not how it looks in the daily schedule.

2. How should the program be structured? Educators may want to start with a simple combined subjects program, or with a conven-tional interdisciplinary team teaching program, but they must realize that these are merely first steps toward the kind of problem-centered core program required to meet present world conditions. Many inter-disciplinary and combined-subjects approaches are burdened with the same emphasis on mastery of subject matter per se that makes con-ventional programs so repelling to students. Educational leaders may need to start where their staff members are, but they must begin at once to help them move toward the core concept. Chapter 9 describes some ways to do it.

Having decided to move toward core, the question remains whether a structured or unstructured program is preferable. Under most circumstances, we recommend a structured core. It provides enough structure so that teachers can do some planning in advance, yet it is open to student input at all stages of the actual study. Parents and other community members know in general what kinds of issues will be examined. Administrators can prepare them for some of the controversial issues that are likely to arise and can establish guidelines to guarantee a free exchange of ideas without unduly antagonizing special interest groups.

3. Should the core class be taught by one teacher or by a team?

This decision depends upon the answer to Question 2. Examination of student problems, values, and concerns, as in core, requires the close rapport between teacher and students that seems best established under the one-teacher plan. In contrast, interdisciplinary teams are often designed to maintain the integrity of each subject while bringing about a modicum of correlation or fusion of content. This is clearly antithetical to core, in which allegiance to subject matter is replaced by commitment to helping students examine problems of both personal and social relevance. Yet, some interdisciplinary team programs may, in time, evolve into core programs, as teachers develop both the competency and the desire to do core teaching. This happened in a number of cases in the early days of the core movement.[14] James Beane has drawn upon the long history of core curriculum to describe the options available to interdisciplinary teams and how to progress toward the core ideal.[15]

Interdisciplinary, team-taught minicourses may be a means to introduce the core idea to a staff, provided that the learning experiences within the course are developed through teacher-student planning, not rigidly prescribed in advance. Consider the possibilities in minicourses such as these, offered at Meadowbrook Junior High School, Newton Centre, Massachusetts: "The World Today," "Coping —Who Am I?" "Dialogue in Black and White," or "Love—Hate." On the other hand, students change minicourses every 9 to 12 weeks, making it difficult for teacher and students to develop the rapport needed for core teaching.

Schools may wish to combine approaches, using the one-teacher model in the lower grades, where the group guidance function of the teacher in most crucial, and then shifting to a team or minicourse approach with older students who may be ready for more formal instruction. Several approaches might function side by side, in recognition that teachers, too, are different. Students who appear to need a more intense, personal relationship with an adult may be placed with a teacher who prefers this pattern; whereas those who need the stimulation of a more complex team operation would have that option. Each approach has its own rewards and demands, so it would be best to allow both teachers and students some choice in the matter. Of course, a student's parents should also be involved in this decision.

4. What instructional techniques should core teachers use? There are no teaching methods that are unique to the core curriculum, although core teachers tend to make greater use of teacher-student planning, small group work, value clarification, and other methods that stress personal interaction. Teachers sometimes find it difficult to enter fully into cooperative planning, since it means relinquishing some of their authority. There may be a temptation to "go through the motions" of teacher-student planning, while in reality manipulating

students to arrive at the decision the teacher wants. On the other hand, teachers may give students too little guidance, allowing them to become bogged down and discouraged with the whole process. Teachers can avoid either extreme if they are sincerely committed to student involvement and willing to work gradually into the teacher-student planning process.

A gradual approach may also be needed if students are not used to small group work. Students working in committees are noisier than a conventional class, but things will not get out of hand if the process has been carefully planned and the students are working on problems they consider worthwhile.[16] Teachers do not need to relinquish their authority to maintain discipline when they share with students some of the decisions on curriculum and instruction.

Core teachers welcome modern individualized approaches to the teaching of basic skills and concepts, such as programmed instruction, learning packages, and computer-assisted-instruction. For example, a number of multimedia "core pacs" are now being used in the core classes of Omaha, Nebraska. Referring students to such sources for content and skill development gives the teacher more time to deal with human relations in the classroom. Yet "prepackaging" an entire program in this fashion should be avoided, lest it fractionate the curriculum, eliminate teacher-student planning, and reduce the inter-action among students and teachers, so vital to the learning process in core.

On the other hand, simulation games, such as *Ghetto* or *Pollution*, seem especially well-suited to the problem-solving emphasis in the core curriculum, and value clarification procedures are extremely useful.[17, 18]

Current techniques for analyzing the teaching process give teachers a powerful tool for reshaping their classroom performance, especially when used with modern videotaping equipment. Since the interaction between teacher and students is especially critical in a core class, core teachers should make frequent use of such schemes as Flanders' Interaction Analysis and its more recent derivatives. They should also keep up with research and experimentation in instruction.[19] Chapter 1 describes some additional resources available for teachers interested in self-improvement.

SUMMARY

Core is recommended as a vehicle for helping middle school students deal with problems of both personal and societal concern under the guidance of a teacher who knows them well. In addition, the core teacher provides a major portion of the day-to-day guidance that is so vital during the transition years. We recommend a structured core taught by one teacher, rather than a team, although interdisciplinary teams or even minicourses may provide a means of introducing the core idea to teachers and students. Chapter 9 discusses staff development approaches needed to implement core or any other curriculum innovation.

References

1. G. F. Vars, ed., *Common Learnings: Core and Interdisciplinary Team Approaches*, (Scranton: International Textbook Company, 1969), pp. 6–10. Portions of this chapter have appeared in *Handbook on Contemporary Education*, edited by Steven E. Goodman. Used with permission of the publisher, R. R. Bowker Company, 1180 Avenue of the Americas, New York. Copyright © 1976 by Xerox Corporation.
2. G. F. Vars, "Curriculum in Secondary Schools and Colleges," *A New Look at Progressive Education*, 1972 Yearbook. (Washington: Association for Supervision and Curriculum Development, 1972), pp. 233–255.
3. G. S. Wright, *Block-Time Classes and the Core Program in the Junior High School*, U.S. Office of Education Bulletin 1958, no. 6. (Washington: Government Printing Office, 1958), p. 15.
4. J. H. Lounsbury and H. R. Douglass, "Recent Trends in Junior High School Practices, 1954–1964," *Bulletin of the National Association of Secondary-School Principals*, (September, 1965), p. 92.
5. National Association for Core Curriculum. *Core Today: Rationale and Implications*, (Kent, Ohio: The Association, 1973).
6. R. M. Zapf, *Democratic Processes in the Secondary Classroom*, (Englewood Cliffs, New Jersey: Prentice-Hall, 1959).
7. L. Parrish and Y. Waskin, *Teacher-Pupil Planning for Better Classroom Learning*, (New York: Pitman, 1967).
8. William Van Til, "What Should Be Taught and Learned Through Secondary Education?" *Issues in Secondary Education*, 75th Yearbook of the National Society for the Study of Education, (Chicago: University of Chicago Press, 1976), pp. 178–214.
9. R. S. Harnack, "Ten Years Later: Research and Development on Computer Based Resource Units," *Educational Technology*, (November, 1976), pp. 7–13.
10. For an elaboration of the guidance function of the teacher see: Ira J. Gordon, *The Teacher as a Guidance Worker*, (New York: Harper and Row, 1956); and P. A. Perrone, T. A. Ryan, and F. R. Zeran, *Guidance and the Emerging Adolescent*, (Scranton, Pa.: International Textbook Company, 1970).
11. G. S. Wright, *The Core Program: Unpublished Research, 1956–1962*, U.S. Office of Education, Circular No. 713. (Washington: Government Printing Office, 1963), p. 11.
12. W. B. Jennings, "Development of the Self-concept in the Core Pro-

gram." Unpublished Ph.D. dissertation, University of Minnesota, 1968. *Dissertation Abstracts,* 1969, 29, 2439A.
13. G. F. Vars, A bibliography of research on the effectiveness of block-time programs. Kent, Ohio: National Association for Core Curriculum, 1974.
14. W. M. Aikin, *The Story of the Eight-Year Study,* (New York: Harper and Row, 1942), pp. 83–85.
15. James A. Beane, "Options for Interdisciplinary Teams," *Dissemination Services on the Middle Grades,* vol. VII, no. 5 (February, 1976), pp. 1–4.
16. L. E. Hock, *Using Committees in the Classroom,* (New York: Holt, Rinehart, and Winston, 1958).
17. L. E. Raths, M. Harmin, and S. B. Simon, *Values and Teaching,* (Columbus, Ohio: Merrill, 1966).
18. Sidney B. Simon, Leland Howe, and Howard Kirshenbaum, *Values Clarification: A Handbook of Practical Strategies for Teachers and Students,* (New York: Hart, 1972).
19. R. S. Soar, "Teacher-Pupil Interaction". *A New Look at Progressive Education,* 1972 Yearbook (Washington: Association for Supervision and Curriculum Development, 1972), pp. 166–204.

6
THE CONTINUOUS PROGRESS COMPONENT

The focus of all education is the individual and his progress. This is accomplished in many classes by allowing a student to work on projects or studies of his own choosing, or by varying either the amount of work or the level of performance expected of different students. Certainly a major appeal of electives and student activities is the opportunities they provide for the individual to "do his own thing."

Yet another approach to individualization is specified in the following guideline, which was derived from our examination of curriculum foundations in Chapter 3: *Every student should have the opportunity to progress at his own rate through a continuous, nongraded sequence of learning experiences in those areas of the curriculum that have a genuine sequential organization.* By "genuine sequential organization" we mean that students must master one set of learnings before they can be expected to succeed at the next level. Sequential learning is most typical of skill areas, such as reading, mathematics, or foreign language. When progress is not tied to age or grade level, we have what is often referred to as a nongraded or ungraded curriculum.

The single-sequence approach

In one type of continuous progress program, all students progress through the same prescribed sequence of learning experiences, but some take more time than others. We refer to this type of program as the *single-sequence, variable-rate approach.*

This is the approach used in most programmed instruction of the linear type. Information is provided in such small quantities or bits that there is virtually no failure, although there may be a problem of boredom if the material is not properly matched to the student's ability and background. The "hardware" of programmed instruction may range from an inexpensive paperback book to the most sophisticated computer. Early claims that the teaching machine would revolutionize education have proved overly optimistic, but instructional materials utilizing the principles of individually paced sequential learning are used in many middle schools.

Most programmed instruction is designed for the student to work by himself, frequently in a study carrel. Since this runs counter to the transescent's drive for peer interaction, it is desirable to specify at various points in the sequence that the student share ideas or data with fellow students.

Most textbook series are based on the single-sequence notion, so many nongraded programs are merely schemes for moving students through the series without regard to conventional grade levels. A commercial system that utilizes this approach is *Individualized Spelling,* available from Research for Better Schools, Inc., Philadelphia. It is based on a more or less conventional set of spelling books published by Follett Publishing Company for grades two through six. Diagnostic tests have been added to these; they are presented by means of a set of cassette tapes and a "management system" designed to help the teacher to individualize instruction. Learning exercises include composition, writing, and reading in addition to spelling.

The Houghton Mifflin Company's *Mathematics for Individual Achievement*[1] is available either as separate booklets or as a conventional hardbound text. In addition to carefully sequenced series of mathematics lessons, the publications include mathematics "labs" and "time outs" that lead students to consider practical applications of the mathematics skills being learned. In Manchester Middle School, near Akron, Ohio, selected students have completed two years of mathematics in one, using these materials, enabling them to take second year mathematics when they go to the high school. Motivation is so high that students sometimes object when work on this program is interrupted by other activities planned by teams of mathematics, science, social studies, and English teachers.

School staff members may accomplish similar results by separating basal textbooks into booklets which are assigned a proficiency level designation. They become self-instructional packets by the addition of self-checking exercises. Thus a seventh grade reading text may be transformed into three packets, perhaps designated levels 15, 16, and 17, to be completed by students in that order. At any one time, students ranging in age from 10 through 15 might be working in the same packet.

Whether based on a textbook series or created independently, learning packets are widely used in middle schools to individualize instruction. Some bear such labels as UNIPAC (Unit Package), LAP (Learning Activity Packet), or TLU (Teaching-Learning Unit). Frequently they specify the behavioral objectives to be achieved and suggest a number of learning activities for the student. Mastery of the contents of one packet, as demonstrated by some kind of test, permits the student to begin the next packet in the series.

Instead of working by himself, a student may be assigned to a class determined by his rate of progress through a learning sequence. Classes are formed on the basis of proficiency levels rather than grade level. This is essentially what happens in the Opportunity Park Middle School described earlier, when all 6th, 7th, and 8th graders in one house have "criterion based instruction" in mathematics or reading at the same time. Sometimes the student moves to the next class when he has mastered the skills or concepts assigned to the class he is in. If the school is large enough, there may be several classes to which he might transfer in order to continue the sequence. This permits the staff to consider other factors in the placement—teacher's personality or favorite teaching mode, the student's learning style or social-emotional maturity, or the predominant age level of students in a class.

Within each clasroom, students move through the learning sequence at their own rate; hence there are students entering or leaving the class at various times throughout the year. Some student interaction is provided, but little continuity of relationships exists.

In view of the labor required to prepare materials for individualized instruction, schools may prefer to buy commercially-prepared sets of materials.[2] Many foreign language laboratory materials provide a single sequence of experiences, as do a good many of the kits, packages, and learning systems in other subject areas.

One of the more sophisticated of the systems is IPI (Individually Prescribed Instruction). IPI was developed by the University of Pittsburgh's Learning Research and Development Center and further refined by Research for Better Schools and by Appleton-Century-Crofts. When IPI was first being introduced, schools that wished to use it were required to purchase the entire system, including a specified amount of in-service training for staff members. Now that more teachers are familiar with individualized approaches to learning, the in-service training is no longer a condition for use of the IPI materials.

IPI reading and mathematics are basically linear programs. IPI mathematics, for example, is built upon a continuum of 359 instructional objectives. Diagnostic tests indicate to the teacher which sets of concepts and skills each student needs to learn. Students are expected to work through the self-instruction booklets in the prescribed order, but they may skip those in which they can demonstrate the necessary competence. Designed for the elementary grades, they have been used above grade six with less capable middle school and junior high students.

The single-sequence approach assumes that educators can agree on the one best sequence for learning. Such a consensus is rarely achieved, even in subjects like reading and mathematics, that have been the focus of intense study and research for many years. Likewise, there are numerous competing foreign language series. Middle school staffs wishing to follow the single-sequence approach will have to choose among many alternatives.

Considering the nature of the transescent, it would seem that approaches which isolate pupils for extended periods of time could generate student antagonisms that might hamper their success. Requiring all students to follow the same sequence is also contrary to what we know about differences in optimum learning style among young people. Therefore we recommend that single-sequence learning materials be used judiciously and only for short periods of time. It should be recognized, however, that such individualized instruction does provide for a modicum of privacy, a rare commodity in most schools and needed to counterbalance the intense preoccupation with peer interaction that characterizes the middle school years.

The multiple-sequence approach

A *multiple-sequence, variable rate* approach to continuous progress provides alternative paths designed by the teacher to accomplish the same objective. The branching form of programmed instruction and the nongraded program advocated by B. Frank Brown[3] are familiar examples of this approach.

In using a branching program, such as a scrambled textbook, the student is presented with information, followed by a quiz. A correct answer enables him to move to the next item in the "main line" of the program. Each incorrect answer guides him to a parallel sequence of learnings designed to correct his misunderstanding and then returns him to the main line.

In B. Frank Brown's form of nongraded program, students are sorted into "phases" according to performance on standardized achievement tests. Students are assigned to phased classes without regard to grade level or age. The curriculum in each phase varies from the basic or remedial to the advanced or "Quest" phase, which is largely independent study. In essence, there are several parallel tracks or ability groups, differing from conventional ability grouping primarily in that students of various ages or grade levels may be working side-by-side in any one class. Students may be shifted from one phase or track to another; consequently all phases must deal with approximately the same subject matter, although on different levels of difficulty. A student who stays in the same phase picks up in September where he left off in June, as in classes arranged in the single-sequence format.

A great deal of time, effort, and expert assistance are needed by a middle school staff to develop a complete multiple-sequence program. Commercial programs are also available. Most educators are familiar with the various kits or "laboratories" in reading, composition, spelling, mathematics, and the like, that have been available for years from publishers such as Science Research Associates. More recently, very sophisticated multi-media systems have become available, such as Westinghouse Learning Corporation's PLAN (Program for Learning in Accordance with Needs) and the High Intensity Learning Center developed by S. Alan Cohen and marketed by Random House.[4]

The HILC-Reading is designed for the first six grades and uses a wide variety of reading development books, kits, programmed materials, and audio-visual materials from many different publishers. Self-instruction is stressed and the student uses only those materials that meet his learning needs, as diagnosed from time to time through tests administered by a teacher or learning center aide. In a fully-equipped High Intensity Learning Center, as many as 50 students may be working on reading skills at the same time, no two of them doing exactly the same thing. A similar system for elementary mathematics is now under development.

In project PLAN, a computer is used to help teachers to keep track of each student's progress. Teachers and students record data on computer cards during the day. These are processed during the night. Next morning, the computer printout shows each child's status, identifies who needs individual help, who is ready for a group discussion, or which student might be able to help a classmate who needs it. Six times a year the computer prints a cumulative record for use in reporting to parents. PLAN systems in language arts (including reading), mathematics, science, and social studies are available through grade eight, after which the school may offer a variety of PLAN individualized high school courses. In mathematics, for example, General Math, Algebra 1, Algebra 2, Geometry, Trigonometry, and Calculus are available. Users of PLAN are expected to participate in the company's workshops for teachers and administrators, the cost of which is included in the package price.

A different computer matching system is being used at the Conwell Magnet Middle School in Philadelphia. In addition to the child's status in the sequence of skills to be mastered, the computer makes allowances for the student's reading and aptitude level, learning style (ability to use and remember information received through visual, auditory, and kinesthetic senses), and cognitive style (strength in learning concrete and abstract relationships.) Utilizing all these variables, the computer matches the student with one of more than 700 learning packets.[5]

Even without the aid of a computer, a teacher can make allowances for individual differences in learning style. For example, a choice can be made between a self-instruction booklet or a sound filmstrip to help a student learn a particular skill. A comparable approach with a foreign language would be to have a variety of language development booklets, tapes, films, filmstrips, and other media available, with the student moving from one to the other according to needs identified by the teacher. It would probably be even better to permit the student to choose, if the alternative learning activities appear equally likely to achieve the desired objective.

Articulation with elementary schools and high schools is a persistent problem in middle schools using either the single-sequence or the multiple-sequence approach. After three years in a middle school, one student may be performing at level 28 in mathematics, another at level 19. Unless the high school mathematics program is also nongraded, the high achiever may be obliged to mark time, while the low achiever may be required to take an extra course, perhaps in summer school, in order to qualify for the first level mathematics course in high school.

Deciding when a student is ready to leave the middle school may also be a problem, especially for a student who has completed the sequence in one area, such as mathematics, but is only part way through the reading sequence. Some schools provide enrichment experiences for advanced students, in order to avoid too great a gap between them and their peers, and extra remedial help for the slower ones, to ensure that both will be ready for transfer to the next school level at about the same time. Either of these approaches should be viewed as a temporary expedient until the entire school system can develop nongraded sequences extending from the lower grades through high school graduation.

A similar problem may occur at the entry level, if elementary and middle schools do not use the same nongraded approach. A middle school committed to continuous progress should be able to take students at whatever level they are functioning and move them ahead at their own individual rates. Ideally, the entire school system should follow the same type of continuous progress program, so that a student can progress at his own rate as long as he is in school. This is symbolized by the jagged lines at the upper ends of the nongraded sequences depicted in Figure 1, page 45.

The variable-sequence approach

Some middle schools have opted for a *variable-sequence, variable-rate* approach to student progress. Here neither the sequence nor the rate is fixed in advance by the teacher. Independent study is an example of this approach. Most independent study projects deal with topics, problems, or content areas rather than the development of skills. It is conceivable, however, for an advanced student in skill subjects such as mathematics or foreign language to be given the option of developing his own sequence of learning experiences under the guidance of a teacher or advisor.

This approach may also be implemented by allowing students to take minicourses or to work in learning packages in any sequence they desire. For example, Individualized Middle Mathematics (IMM), currently under development by Research for Better Schools, gives seventh and eighth grade students many options. They may choose the order in which units are studied, select which special learning activities to do, decide whether to work independently or in small groups, and determine when to seek help from the teacher. In this system the student's entry point, his rate of progress, and his sequence of experiences are all individualized.

Like the two approaches described previously, the variable-sequence, variable-rate approach results in students of various ages working in the same learning package or minicourse. Time variation in the minicourse approach comes from the number of minicourses a student is required to complete, rather than in the length of time he spends in each minicourse. For example, the school may require each student to take a minimum of twelve nine-week minicourses in English over a three year period, but some students may take as many as fourteen or fifteen.

In the skill areas, most schools impose some control on learning sequence, if only by requiring all students to take certain basic minicourses or learning packages early in their school careers. Another approach is to establish prerequisites. For example, in Roosevelt Junior High School, Eugene, Oregon, the minicourse in Speech is prerequisite to the one in Debate, and an 18-week mathematics course labeled "Orientation" is prerequisite to such minicourses as "Metric and Nonmetric Geometry" or "Ratio, Proportion, Decimals, and Percent." Moreover, it is suggested that students with a reading problem take "Phonics in Reading and Spelling," followed by "Vocabulary Building" and/or "Reading Speed and Comprehension."

Some schools exclude the basic skills entirely from the minicourse format, offering minicourses only in enrichment topics, such as Computer Mathematics, Topology, Speed Reading, or Latin American Literature. Minicourses and other elective experiences will be dealt with more fully in the next chapter.

The multi-unit approach

The multiage unit plan, while sometimes heralded as an approach to continuous progress, really focuses on student grouping rather than on curriculum structure. One widely promoted example is IGE, Individually Guided Education. This plan groups several teachers and students of different age levels into a "unit", with the stipulation that the staff diagnose individual student needs and then plan curriculum experiences to meet those needs. Ways of organizing staff and pupils are suggested, but curricular decisions are left in the hands of the teaching team. Thus, a team may use any or all of the curricular approaches to continuous progress described above, or even elect to teach students in conventional classes, where appropriate.

Since new students enter the unit and older ones leave it each year, the major topics or problems studied by the entire group must be rotated. For example, in social studies, a three-year middle school may engage the students in studying Latin America one year, Africa the next, and Asia the next, returning to Latin America again the fourth year. Skill development cannot be tied directly to these units, because students would encounter the skills in different order depending upon at what point in the cycle they entered the middle school. Once the rudiments of a skill are mastered, however, sequence does not appear to be so critical. This is illustrated in some of the PLAN sequences and in the decision of the Research for Better Schools staff to follow IPI Mathematics, which is essentially linear, with IMM, which offers many options.

Recommendations

We have already cautioned against excessive use of continuous progress plans that keep students isolated from each other for extended periods of time. Nor is there much to be gained by taking traditional irrelevant content and breaking it down into hundreds of small assignments. As Westbury aptly puts it, "Instead of the tyranny of the teacher, we have the tyranny of the ditto machine; math or reading becomes the filling in of little spaces—without discussion, manipulation, or demonstration."[6] Any individualized, continuous progress learning sequence must be geared to the needs of the learner as a total person.

There are also drawbacks inherent in forming groups of various ages and maturities. Regardless of how the staff may try to rationalize it, a founrteen-year-old is likely to feel "stupid" if he is working on reading or mathematics skills in a group consisting primarily of eleven and twelve-year-olds. If the school is large enough, skill grouping can be formed on both performance level *and* maturity level to minimize this factor. If the membership in each group shifts frequently, and the grouping is clearly based on performance rather than some measure of presumed intelligence, these groups may avoid the social stigma attached to conventional ability groups. Another approach is to establish learning centers in which students of all ages are working on a multitude of levels.

Nongraded approaches that permit the student to choose those with whom he works at a particular proficiency level are even better. A student may end up working with a younger student, but at least it is his choice. Our experience has been that younger students tend to seek association with older or more socially mature students, whereas many of the older ones resent having to associate with "little kids." As nongraded or multiage groupings become more prevalent, these antagonisms may diminish, but they are not likely to disappear. In striving for maturity, young people often reject things, people, and ideas that they associate with their younger years.

It is our recommendation that middle schools use multiple-sequence, variable-rate programs to provide those learnings in which sequence has been clearly demonstrated to be critical. These would appear to be the rudiments of reading, mathematics, foreign languages, and possibly some of the process skills in science.

The basic approach should be one of individual diagnosis, with each student being provided the type of learning sequence that best meets his needs. As skills are mastered, the student should be given more and more options, thus gaining increasing control over his own learning.

Throughout this "intellectual weaning" process, there should be ample time for students to interact with others who are working at a similar level and to help those less skilled. Whenever possible, the student should have some choice of the learning mode to be used. In contrast to the core program, where stability and continuity are desired, student groupings for these learnings should be flexible, to minimize any suggestion of permanent ability grouping.

The learnings in the nongraded skill development area should be reinforced throughout the school program. All teachers, guidance counselors, and activity advisors must accept responsibility for helping students improve their skills whenever and wherever they are applied. This is symbolized by the use of dotted lines between the nongraded sequences and other aspects of the program in Figure 1, page 45.

SUMMARY

Middle school educators have several options available for providing instruction in those skill areas where sequence is crucial. Single-sequence, variable-rate approaches may be used with individual students or with overlapping class groupings. These programs are perhaps the easiest to design, but they are based on the questionable assumption that all students can learn best through one sequence of experiences.

Multiple-sequence, variable-rate approaches offer the learner more options, while still keeping control of the sequence in the hands of the professional educator. Since such programs may resemble tracking systems, caution must be taken to avoid stigmatizing students. Designing multiple sequences is a difficult process.

Variable-sequence, variable-rate approaches place control of the sequence in the hands of the student; therefore, they should be used only after the student has mastered the rudiments of a skill. The multiage unit is a means of organizing staff and students, rather than a curricular structure. Skill development in a multiage unit may be carried out with any of the above approaches, as well as through conventional class instruction.

The authors believe that the multiple-sequence, variable-rate approach best reconciles the need for sequential skill development with individual differences in learning style. Students should be weaned from these prescribed sequences as rapidly as possible so that they may assume more and more control of their learning.

References

1. Richard A. Denholm, Donald D. Hankins, Marian Cliffe Herrick, and George R. Voitko, *Mathematics for Individual Achievement*, (Boston: Houghton Mifflin, 1975).

2. See: Ronald E. Hull, "Selecting an Approach to Individualized Education," *Phi Delta Kappan*, vol. 55, no. 3 (November, 1973), pp. 169–173.
3. B. Frank Brown, *The Nongraded High School*, (Englewood Cliffs, N.J.: Prentice-Hall, 1963); *The Appropriate Placement School: A Sophisticated Nongraded Curriculum*, (West Nyack, N.Y.: Parker, 1965).
4. See: S. Alan Cohen, *Teach Them All to Read*, (New York: Random House, 1969).
5. John A. Connolly, "Basic Education—A Mastery Approach," *Phi Delta Kappan*, vol. 54, no. 3 (November, 1972), pp. 211–212.
6. Ian Westbury, "Leap from Blackboard to Ditto Sheet Is Not a Great Movement," *Phi Delta Kappan*, vol. 58, no. 7 (March, 1976), p. 482. (A review of *Systems of Individualized Education*, ed. Harriet Talmadge. Berkeley, Calif.: McCutchan, 1975.)

THE VARIABLE COMPONENT: EXPLORATION AND ACTIVITIES

The third component of the curriculum organization outlined in Chapter 4 is labeled "variable," because learning experiences within this component are structured in a variety of ways. Certain elective minicourses may be problem-centered and developed through teacher-student planning, similar to a core class. Skill development in music or art may be carefully sequenced and highly individualized, as in the continuous progress component. But neither of these approaches dominates the vast array of courses, activities, clubs, and independent study opportunities that round out a good middle school curriculum.

Student groupings and time allotments also vary within this component. There may be year-long physical education courses, mini-courses that last six to nine weeks, and independent study projects that may be completed in a few days. Formality of organization may vary widely. At one extreme would be a tightly disciplined school orchestra or a student council run strictly according to *Roberts' Rules of Order*. At the other would be a highly informal mixed faculty-student basketball game during lunch or after school. Perhaps it is

this component of the curriculum that comes closest to mirroring the
bewildering transcience and diversity of the transescent student. Offerings in this component provide many of the common learnings needed
by all students as well as individualized experiences geared to each
student's uniqueness. All of the guidelines derived in Chapter 3 apply
to this component, but primary emphasis is on the concept of exploration. As Guideline 4 states: *Every student should have access to a rich
variety of exploratory experiences, both required and elective.*

The concept of exploration was one of the original junior high
school bywords. Since it is directly related to many characteristics and
needs of early adolescents, it has continued as a primary feature of
middle school education. Middle schools, in fact, have given renewed
emphasis to exploration and have encouraged experimentation with
various nontraditional exploratory and enrichment experiences.

Originally, the concept of exploration was rather restricted; it
referred primarily to familiarizing students with new subject areas in
order to eventually make wise decisions regarding high school electives
and/or vocational pursuits. Today, exploration is viewed much more
broadly, as a point of view or a process, not just as specific exploratory
"content." It may be fostered in required general education courses
such as science or physical education, as well as in short-term foreign
language or business courses. Much of the work in a core class is
clearly exploratory, both in content and in process. Wherever and
whenever provided, however, exploration is a manifestation of the
middle school's commitment to help young people to know themselves,
their interests, aptitudes, and capabilities, and to satisfy their natural
curiosity and questing.

The specific elements in this curriculum component will vary
according to how a particular school defines and delineates the elements. However organized, the portions usually are: health and
physical education, required exploratory courses, special interest
courses, independent study, and student activities.

Health and physical education

The marked physical growth of young people during the middle
school years, together with attendant health concerns, have earned
this area a firm place in any middle school curriculum. It is required
of all students because of the vital common learnings it provides,
and it also offers a rich array of exploratory experiences. What passes
for physical education may be provided through playground recess
in the elementary school and optional physical activity periods at the
secondary level, but few would advocate such a hit-or-miss approach

at the intermediate level. Usually the area is given the equivalent of a period each day of the week every year, although sometimes it alternates with electives or exploratory experiences.

A comprehensive health and physical education program for the middle school includes: (1) required physical education classes for all boys and girls with accompanying instruction in skills and rules; (2) organized instruction in health education, first aid, and safety education; and (3) an intramural athletics program essentially involving all students. Some limited forms of interschool athletic activities may be a part of the program, although varsity-type programs are usually judged inappropriate for middle school youngsters. Responsibility for school camping and outdoor education may also be delegated to the physical education staff, although these programs ideally embrace nearly all aspects of the curriculum.

Physical education classes. The regular physical education classes should include movement training, body building exercises, a wide variety of individual and dual activities, team games, and related large and small group instruction. Activities which have clear carry-over values, such as golf, bowling, ping pong, badminton, folk dancing, and swimming, should be emphasized. Middle school youngsters need physical activities that help them develop skills and coordination rather than those that reveal and emphasize their lack of skill and poor coordination. Consider the impact on a developing transescent's self-image when required to compete with more capable peers in highly competitive team sports like basketball, football, or baseball. Instead, personal satisfaction and recognition of progress should result from physical education activities, hence the increasing emphasis on individual and dual sports.

Middle schools are experimenting with a number of different formats for providing learning experiences in this area. Many physical education activities can be conducted in coeducational groups, thereby meeting both social and physical needs. Volleyball, tennis, folk and square dancing, bowling, table tennis, and badminton are among activities appropriate for mixed groups.

Some schools offer physical education minicourses and allow students to switch every few weeks. For example, in one middle school, eighth and ninth graders selected from among the following options, which changed every five weeks: bowling, basketball, gymnastics, fitness, swimming, softball, archery, track and field.

The Intramural Program. This portion of the program builds on the skills learned in the instructional program. It is usually separate from the physical education program, although it is the responsibility of physical education faculty members. Ideally, all boys and girls will participate in some of the varied types of intramural competition. Individual, dual, and team sports are all necessary. In some schools recreational activities such as checkers are available to supplement the more competitive intramural activities. Many of these may also be offered as electives or student activities.

Health education. Health instruction may be provided in core, science, homemaking, or physical education classes, or in all four, or in a separate course. At the intermediate level, health is too important to suffer the neglect that often befalls something that is "everybody's business." Rapidly maturing early adolescents need help in understanding their changing bodies, the varied rates and times of such changes, and aspects of human sexuality. Community health services, drugs, alcohol, tobacco, and diet are key topics deserving planned instruction.[1]

Every middle school needs at least one professionally prepared health educator to guide the school's efforts in this vital area. Working with this coordinator would be a health team consisting of the school nurse, a representative of the guidance department, and teachers of core, science, home economics, and physical education. If the school has an effective core program, the team would probably decide to delegate most health instruction to the core class, with support and reinforcement from the other areas. A separate health course may make it possible for staff members to develop special competence in this area, but it is very likely to become isolated from the other life issues being dealt with elsewhere in the school program. The goal is to give continuing attention to students' physical, social, and emotional health needs throughout their years in the middle school.

Interscholastic athletics. The place of interscholastic athletics in the middle school remains a matter of some controversy. Generally, competition between schools has been opposed on at least two counts: (1) the widely-shared belief that middle school youngsters simply have not reached a point of physical development and maturation that makes intensive competition and contact advisable;[2] and (2) the feeling that it is precisely on this issue that the junior high school too often imitates the high school, thereby losing much of its unique educational mission. Yet, in today's athletically oriented society, it is hard to rule out all interschool competition. Many feel that given adequate direction and control, some competition is healthy and meets a real need of a portion of the student body.[3] Former junior high schools converting to middle schools may have found the long-standing community expectation of interscholastic athletics at the intermediate level almost too strong to counter.

Some schools have a "no cut" rule which guarantees that anyone who comes out for a team will play in every game. Others find the "play day" idea more satisfactory, in which boys and girls from different schools get together for competition in a variety of sports, often with the membership of each team drawn from all participating schools.

The Marlington Middle School of Alliance, Ohio, may be cited for its well-coordinated intramural-interscholastic program. Ninety-five per cent of the student body engage in one or more intramural programs, a commendable figure. A combination of individual, coed, and team sports are scheduled during lunch periods, after school, and on Saturdays. All team members play at least half a game, and no one is dropped from a squad. The same coaches supervise both intramural teams and the interscholastic teams which evolve from them.[4]

Intramural sports at Marlington include flag football, girls' soccer, volleyball (coed), basketball, floor hockey, track, and softball. Interscholastic competition is provided in contact football (7th and 8th grade boys), basketball (boys and girls) and track (boys and girls).

Outdoor education. This area is discussed here because it is often considered a part of the health and physical education program. However, outdoor education cuts across all subject areas, and could just as well have been included in the chapter on core. Note how much the definition of outdoor education which follows, overlaps with the concepts of core.

Four of the movement's leaders have offered these sentences as a response to the question, "What is outdoor education?"

> Outdoor education is a means of curriculum enrichment through experiences in and for the outdoors. It is not a separate discipline with prescribed objectives like science and mathematics, it is simply a learning climate which offers opportunities for direct laboratory experiences in identifying and resolving real-life problems, for acquiring skills with which to enjoy a lifetime of creative living, for attaining concepts and insights about human and natural resources, and for getting us back in touch with those aspects of living where our roots were once firmly established.[5]

Outdoor education should not be classified as an educational innovation, for it has been a feature of many school programs since the 1920s. The area, however, has been experiencing a kind of renaissance in the last ten or fifteen years. The national concern for the environment and the renewed emphasis by educators on laboratory type experiences, open education, and more relevant educational activities are among the factors which have sparked this rapid expansion. Many state legislatures and state boards of education have taken official action in support of outdoor education.

The middle school years are, in many respects, the most appropriate years for school-sponsored outdoor education activities. In practice, these years are probably the most commonly involved years. Here, a high degree of curiosity, with adequate mental maturity and clear needs for socialization, combine to make school camping meaningful and effective. Residential programs which continue over several days and nights in a field site are especially desirable. Often learning about human relationships in such settings is as meaningful as the many diverse lessons relating to the outdoors.

Schools which have no access to a camp, lodge, or similar facility need not, however, pass up outdoor education. Any school ground or campus is a laboratory that can be used as a resource. Nature trails can be developed. The help of county agents, local recreation association personnel, and science teachers is often readily available and freely offered. Though the physical education or core teacher may act as leader, an entire middle school staff can be utilized in the cooperative planning for such an adventure in education. Indeed, there is hardly an area or a school subject that is not naturally a part of the study of the outdoors *in* the outdoors.

Required exploratory courses

In intermediate schools, the subjects most often classified as exploratory are: music, art, home economics, and industrial arts. These important areas have most typically been provided through required one semester courses at one grade level, with electives available at other grade levels. Traditionally, boys took industrial arts while girls took homemaking. However, "exchange units" that give boys several weeks of cooking and girls an equal length of time in "home mechanics" have been provided over the years in some schools. A substantial and still growing number of schools enroll both boys and girls in the same classes, as sex stereotypes vanish, a result of federal regulations and the long overdue movement for women's rights.

Sex distinctions are practically eliminated in unified arts programs, in which both boys and girls have simultaneous access to art, home economics, and industrial arts facilities. For example, a visit to the related arts suite in Hemlock (Michigan) Middle School revealed approximately ninety youngsters working on various projects. A group of boys and girls had a "production line" going, cooking tacos for sale to other students and faculty. Both boys and girls were using sewing machines, making hooked rugs, drawing, making pottery, and using shop equipment. Teachers moved from area to area, helping individuals and small groups.

Exploratory music is primarily concerned with appreciation rather than performing, hence optional activities in band and chorus for interested and/or talented students are usually provided in addition to the required general music course. Exploratory music, on the other hand, aims simply to make all students comfortable with music, allowing them to freely enjoy it, both as participants and as listeners. At the same time it meets some of the socialization needs of transescents. Widely accepted in theory, this approach sometimes is lost in implementation. Too often music specialists seem unable to teach music except with the goals of perfection and performing typical of a high school music department. This situation is improving as middle schools include music in exploratory unified arts program and colleges prepare music teachers who are more aware of the special needs of transescents.

Art is also a means of providing creative expression and developing appreciation instead of primarily refining talents. Art is an area whose importance extends far beyond the obvious and very important aesthetic and creative expression aspects. Art is an ally of the two major middle school responsibilities—skill development and personal development. It can contribute directly to both better reading and better self-concepts. Probably art has the potential of being the most complete and theoretically correct laboratory of learning of any instructional area. Here each individual, as an individual, has the opportunity to express thoughts and feelings without reference to right or wrong, good or bad. Middle schools should take great care to utilize fully this basic exploratory area.

Home economics, more appropriately labeled homemaking, gives direct attention to such relevant concerns as child care and babysitting, nutrition, party planning, consumer education, and personal grooming. While some of these topics are appropriate for boys and girls, there may well be a place in the exploratory program for a few "girls only" experiences as well as coed ones.

Industrial arts deals with such topics as technology in American life, plastics, the metric system, wood finishing, use of handtools and home repairs. Once considered a dumping ground for those unable to do "brainwork," industrial arts has a major role in our technological society. Likewise, in a society with considerable leisure time and an emphasis on do-it-yourself, the area has considerable carry over value.

These four basic areas, when treated as exploratory courses, are valid as general education and should be required of all. Taught in laboratory situations, with considerable hands-on experiences, these areas are popular with emerging adolescents. It is advantageous to provide opportunities in these exploratory areas at more than one grade or maturity level, but normally they need not be provided every year for all pupils. Many middle schools adopt a type of program whereby longer periods of time are provided at higher grade levels for those who select the area. For instance, all sixth graders might take six weeks of art appreciation, seventh graders might elect art as one of several nine-week courses, while eighth graders might elect a full semester of art.

Electives

Electives have always been a means of meeting individual interests and providing for exploration. Typical electives are: general business, personal typing, modern foreign language, band or chorus, and algebra (as opposed to general math). Occasionally a special science course, such as earth science, biology, or physical science, may be available as an alternate to general science. Remedial work also is often provided in the "elective" block. As pointed out in Chapter 6, electives may be part of a nongraded or continuous progress sequence.

Electives are usually distinguishable from special interest enrichment courses by the manner in which they are credited on the record and by the marking procedures employed. That is, they "count" toward graduation, and students earn the same kinds of marks as in the required English, social studies, or core courses.

Some middle schools have launched a "quarter" system in which the usual nine months course is divided into three quarters, with a summer quarter as the optional fourth quarter. Students register each quarter so that class membership may shift considerably from quarter to quarter. At the least innovative degree, a course such as eighth grade English may remain essentially unchanged, except that is is now divided into three quarters rather than two semesters. Failing students may repeat a particular nine-week segment without losing the entire year. At its best, each quarter may be a genuine minicourse, with completely different and more relevant content. Such a plan may offer greater flexibility of scheduling for students and better utilization of teacher competence. However, as a major curriculum reorganization proposal for the middle school, the minicourse approach creates the sequencing problems discussed in Chapter 6. It also perpetuates the focus of educational effort on content, regardless of how it is packaged, and on "courses" of whatever length.

As more extensive and flexible programs of exploratory and enrichment courses are developed, and as ninth grades are increasingly being located in the high school, regular electives of a semester or a year's duration are becoming less prevalent. Some middle schools provide no formal elective courses. Instead, students "elect" or choose numerous minicourses, projects, or learning sequences of varying length.

Interest-centered enrichment courses

To supplement the required exploration in areas such as art, music, homemaking and industrial arts, schools usually provide a series of interest-centered short courses. These courses are also frequently referred to as minicourses, since they tend to be of short duration—four to nine weeks. Unlike the short courses offered to meet exploratory requirements, these courses usually bear titles that indicate a specific and limited focus rather than a subject label. Conventional marks are seldom used, and content is often openly recreational, with emphasis on "hands-on" experiences.

The Northwest Middle School of Greenville, South Carolina, for instance, has an extensive special interest program which involves all students daily during the last period. Students select, with parental concurrence, the "Special Interest Classes" they desire each six weeks. Courses are not graded and most are open to students without regard for grade level. Classes meet for 45 minutes. An individual student, during a school year, will engage in at least six activities.

These activity classes run the gamut from academic enrichment to purely recreational. Among the nearly fifty classes provided are: Bridge, Crochet, Advanced Math, Afghan Making, Basketball Skills, Chess, Child Care, Creative Writing, Cross Country, Environmental Education, First Aid, Horseshoes, Improve Your Handwriting, Newspaper, Speed Reading, Volleyball Officiating, and Wordo (a vocabulary building game).

The courses offered are determined on the basis of student interests and faculty competencies. Changes in these courses occur regularly. This selection and registration involve considerable time and effort, but results in full and varied participation more than justify the expenditure, according to Principal Norman Harris.

The Middle Schools of the Lindberg School District, St. Louis, Missouri, instituted a rather complex exploratory program which ultimately utilized a computer to assist in registering students in activities of their choice. The schools alternate a seven period day with an eight period day. Exploratory courses meet in this eighth period, three days one week and two days the next. Activities change after twelve weeks, or thirty meetings. First, faculty members indicated three activities they would be willing to sponsor. This compilation was then submitted to students who indicated first, second, and third choices. While the nearly sixty activities are varied, they are predominantly recreational and non-academic, with Pet Training, Desk Football, Boxing, Creative Stitchery, Paint-by-Numbers, and Record Club typical.[6]

The Wilbur Wright Middle School of Munster, Indiana, has combined many of the usual required exploratory experiences and a variety of special interest enrichment courses in a comprehensive program called Unified Arts. Seventy minicourses are offered, each of three weeks' duration. Students take six each semester or twelve per year in the 6th, 7th, and 8th grades, for a total of 36. Some of the elections each year must be in the areas of home, applied, and fine arts. For example, home arts comprise baking, snacks and desserts, needlepoint, and rugmaking; applied arts include foundry, woods, electricity, and crafts; fine arts offer printmaking, macrame, ceramics, and design. Students can advance through three levels of any given course such as Ceramics I, Ceramics II, and Ceramics III.[7] The six staff members, former "specialists" in art, home economics, and industrial arts, handle the scheduling and work as a team.

The middle schools of Madison, Wisconsin, have a similar exploratory program which is also called Unified Arts. One major difference is the provision of a block of laboratory time, 80 minutes two or three times a week. Students explore the three areas of art, home economics, and industrial arts in each of the three grades (6, 7, and 8). The classes are team taught and students are involved in many decisions, particularly in the laboratory sessions.[8]

The possibilities for short term interest-centered courses are literally endless. Fads in fashion, transportation, gadgets, and TV game shows, can lead to courses such as leather work, skateboard safety, fun with pocket calculators, CB radio, or "Concentration." Faculty talents and hobbies are also major determinants of possibilities. So too are geographical factors which might give rise to classes in mountain climbing in one area and waterskiing in another.

Independent study

The ultimate aim of formal education is the development of independent learners. "The job of the teacher," Elbert Hubbard pointed out long ago, "is to make himself unnecessary." In a time when we are literally drowning in new knowledge, when coverage of important information is openly acknowledged to be an impossible task, it can be said that only those who know *how* to learn know enough. If such views are valid it could well be asked, "How can independent learners be developed if students are never given opportunities to learn independently?"

Unfortunately, independent study is still considered by many to be a learning procedure that is reserved for high school honors students and college students. Yet, independent study projects may vary in complexity and challenge, the simpler ones well within the capabilities of elementary school students. Independent study may be difficult to implement primarily because formal schooling, carried on almost exclusively in teacher-dominated classes, has created dependent learners. Despite much rhetoric about developing independent learners, most schools still overplay the role of the student as a passive receiver of education, while underplaying the role of the student as an active agent responsible for his own learning. Neither teachers nor students are sufficiently cognizant of the potential for self-instruction that resides in all humans. Leading middle schools are beginning to tap that potential.

The term, independent study, is subject to many interpretations. Used loosely, it could be applied to almost all homework assignments. In their research study, Alexander and Hines developed a more restricted definition of independent study:

> Independent study is considered by us to be learning activity largely motivated by the learner's own aims to learn and largely rewarded in terms of its intrinsic values. Such activity as carried on under the auspices of secondary schools is somewhat independent of the class or other group organization dominant in past and present secondary school instructional practices, and it utilizes the services of teachers and other professional personnel primarily as resources for the learner.[9]

Independent study takes many forms. Core teachers frequently utilize it as one of the varied types of activities needed in problem-centered teaching. Independently pursued projects may be an option in exploratory programs. Sometimes it is an alternate to formal instruction in basic courses for advanced students. At times independent study is formalized in a contract which stipulates the conditions of the agreement and is signed by the student, a teacher/advisor, and perhaps the parents. Preplanned packages and units, although used by individuals in an independent manner, are not normally considered to provide independent study experience.

In the Beachwood, Ohio, Middle School, a comprehensive independent study program is operated by the interdisciplinary teams into which this open space school is divided. Called Personalized Educational Activities (P.E.A.), this program was developed as a means of achieving the stated objectives of individualizing and personalizing learning opportunities. A P.E.A. is self-selected and rewarded only in terms of its own values. Projects do not tend to be of the library research type so commonly utilized in independent study. Examples are: spending four weeks with a kidney specialist engaging in animal research at Mt. Sinai Hospital; producing an eleven minute sound film detailing the processes of steel fabrication; investigating architecture and design, including six weeks of working with architects, construction workers, and other practitioners in the field; and a research-oriented study of local transportation with suggested solutions. Students keep journals, confer periodically with teachers, and are expected to present a result or outcome, which may take such forms as an oral defense, visual display, or written report.[10]

Student activities

It is in the area of student activities that middle schools are most likely to fall prey to the disease that infects many junior highs—imitating the high school. Interscholastic athletics, marching bands, performing musical groups, and formal dances are the tempting avenues for inappropriately reproducing the more mature and sophisticated high school ways. Yet the needs of middle school youngsters for clubs, organizations, and social activities cannot and should not be ignored.

Even though comprehensive exploratory programs do absorb many of the learning experiences usually found in activity programs, such programs cannot meet all the needs. Exploratory courses are just that—courses—with teacher leadership, however informal, dedicated to achieving certain objectives. Student activities, on the other hand, are normally run by students with the teacher serving more as an advisor or facilitator. Intramural programs, student government, service clubs, and parties are among the valid activities that are not likely to be provided in an exploratory-enrichment program.

To say that a distinct and separate activity program is needed to provide necessary learning experiences is to acknowledge, at least in part, that something is wrong with, or missing in, the "regular" classes, which is frequently the case. The ideal school would probably have no division at all between class and extraclass, course and student activity, regular "academics" and social/recreational experiences. The elimination of such separateness will take many years, but the middle school may well be the best place to begin. Certainly, for early adolescents the educational experiences commonly associated with activity programs are central and not to be considered frills or peripheral. Opportunities for leadership, self-management, responsibility, socialization, pursuit of aptitudes and interests—these are important aspects of middle school education.

Clubs and student organizations

Many exploratory enrichment classes are designated as clubs, such as Chess Club, and unfortunately many clubs are operated like regular classes. The distinction between clubs and classes may be blurred, but there are, or should be, differences. Clubs should be largely directed by student officers; they should include as members all who choose to join; and they should extend for a longer period of time than most minicourses. The need to belong and to be a part of a group of peers is so important to emerging adolescents that it is better met in a somewhat formally organized club than it is in a short-term activity class, even when that class is self-selected.

Although the need for cultivating interests may be met by a broad exploratory program, service clubs meet other needs. Young adolescents have humanitarian and social service concerns that ought to be cultivated. Organizations which have a service function can capitalize on the natural idealism of early adolescents. Junior Red Cross, Library, Audio-Visual Aides, Future Teachers, and the School Newspaper are examples of service-oriented organizations.

Student government. While student government is a type of social service club, it warrants special attention. An effective student government is the cornerstone of a citizenship development program. In a democracy the provision of a positive, practical, political education is certainly mandated by society. Whether the usual school student council can provide this education is another matter. Cuff has forcefully dealt with this issue. After making a strong case for student participation in government he concludes: "Too often have intermediate schools responded to the need of their students for political education with the student council charade."[11] He believes that "a school wide organization is probably counter-productive in all but the smallest intermediate school. Unfamiliarity with the students outside one's own classroom sharply limits the possibility of rational choice of school leaders. A great deal about which students have legitimate voice occurs within grades rather than at the building level. . . . Leadership concentrated at the school level precludes widespread leadership experience."[12]

Cuff proposes adapting the size of the school political unit with which students are involved to their maturity. For fifth and sixth graders this means the individual class or section. At the seventh grade, the "house" (school-within-a-school or wing) might be the basis; while at the eighth grade level the entire grade might become the political unit. He also advocates a more direct attempt at teaching the principles of self-governance. Here the core program is especially well-suited to underpin a student government organization. The core class provides a meaningful basis for representation and reporting as well as an appropriate situation for teaching principles of self-government.

Middle school youngsters are capable of carrying out a program of student government. It is easy, but incorrect, to underestimate their ability to be serious or to think deeply. A student government organization can secure student reaction to the curriculum, plan social activities, and coordinate the club program. Conducting cleanup campaigns, assisting community welfare organizations, raising money for overseas relief, fostering school spirit, and developing standards of conduct, are other matters that may well be the province of student government.

Guidelines for a middle school activity program

The following guidelines are prepared to help educators garner the maximum benefits from a student activities program:

1. *Time for student activities must be provided on a regular basis within the school day.* The importance of student activities to the achievement of middle school objectives makes any other arrangement unacceptable. While a separate and designated activity period is certainly logical and an accepted arrangement, it is not the only workable plan. In some middle schools, the core class provides the locus of various activities. In addition to student government, they include homeroom meetings and intramural athletics.

There are, of course, a few activities that will and should be scheduled after school. Some intramurals, social activities, major dramatic productions, and special musical events frequently require additional time, but these can be considered exceptions.

2. *Participation in middle school activities should not be restricted on the grounds of academic achievement, financial status, or social standing.* Again, a few individual exceptions may be in order, such as a club for advanced foreign language students; but there is no valid basis for applying a blanket eligibility requirement such as a C average. A carry-over from the time when activities were "extra-curricular" frills added to an otherwise rigorous academic program, such restrictions on participation simply do not belong in a middle

school, in which activities are a primary means of achieving educational objectives.

3. *The specific activities and organizations included in the program should remain open and easy to change.* A highly formalized program of clubs, replete with constitutions and by-laws, is not likely to meet the shifting and ephemeral needs of transescents. Though a few clubs may carve out a continuing niche for themselves and justify their perpetuation, on the whole, student organizations will and should change frequently. New students bring new interests; new faculty do likewise. The end of an organization ought to be treated as natural, not a failure.

4. *Sponsorship of activities should be considered integral to a teacher's job rather than as an extra assignment.* Whether or not additional pay is received will depend upon local policies and conditions. In any case, these responsibilities should be viewed as vital parts of a professional middle school teacher's assignment.

5. *Students can and should play a role in developing, operating, and regulating activity programs.* This does *not* eliminate the need for comparable responsibilities in the subject or core classes. However, in activity programs, student input is especially important and quite readily accepted and implemented. The student council or a student-faculty committee might serve as the primary supervisor of an activity program.

6. *The nature, extent, and purposes of the activity program should be fully understood by each faculty member.* This will enhance support of the program, and of greater importance, bring about a fuller realization of the significance of activities to the achievement of the objectives of the middle school.

Scheduling and staffing

Schools vary widely in the way they schedule and staff this part of the school program. Courses or activities may be three, four, six, or nine weeks in duration. Classes or meetings may be 30, 40, or 50 minutes in length and scheduled anywhere from one to five times a week.[13] All school staff members may be involved, from principal to school custodian, as well as parents and other adults from the community and students from nearby high schools and colleges.

The readiness of the student body and the faculty, the existing traditions, and the time constraints imposed by other aspects of the curriculum, are among variables which can and should be considered. This should *not* imply that exploratory courses and activities are of little importance, or that they can easily "make do" with whatever time is left over from the "real stuff" of the curriculum. It *is* to say that so many variables must be considered that no hard and fast rules regarding time can be advocated as universally appropriate for this area of the curriculum.

One important factor to be considered is the richness of the cultural and exploratory experiences provided to students outside of the school. In wealthy suburbs, students may be heavily involved in activities sponsored by parents, churches, synagogues, YM and YWCA's, country clubs, and the like. A relatively modest exploratory program may be all that is needed to supplement these experiences. On the other hand, in impoverished areas, both rural and urban, the school may be expected to assume a great deal of responsibility for enriching the lives of both children and adults.

Some exploratory experiences can be one-time independent activities rather than parts of a continuous program. Resident outdoor education programs, for instance, may involve a portion of the school for three or four days at a time. Extensive field trips to planetariums or museums may involve whole grades for a day, irrespective of what courses they may be enrolled in. In a Kent, Ohio, middle school, students spend a "day at work" with one of their parents as part of a career orientation unit. A Tallahassee, Florida, middle school provided "a day in school out of school" as an enrichment exploratory experience for the entire student body. A major shopping center served as the physical site for this particular day, with the various merchants becoming specialized resource people and teachers.

A few middle schools seek to meet some of the exploratory needs of pupils and also to enrich the standard curriculum offerings by providing a bi-weekly or monthly "smorgasbord" day. Utilizing the basic format of the "Study Day" which has been employed in some high schools for more than twenty years,[14] these schools plan a variety of options and activities for this "scatter" day. Regular classes do not meet; instead the faculty are available to direct special activities, conduct field trips, supervise independent study, provide make-up work, and sponsor particular organizations. Community resource people are frequently brought in to present programs. A special schedule showing the period and the options is prepared and distributed. Each student builds his own schedule for the day, usually under teacher guidance.

As important as these experiences may be, there is danger that middle schools may overemphasize exploratory courses and activities. They may falsely assume that having a large number of interesting activities, no matter how trivial many of them may be, will adequately insure meeting all the exploratory objectives of the middle school. This is particularly true in schools without a core program or its equivalent.

A problem-centered program such as core, provides a continuous, stable group where the deliberate and orderly consideration of many issues and concerns can take place. Values clarification, career exploration, human relationships, and self-development are examples of important exploratory experiences that both can and should be provided within the regular academic portion of the curriculum. Fundamental skill development should not be neglected in order to expand exploratory offerings. A balance among all three major curriculum components is the goal.

SUMMARY

The third component of the curriculum design recommended by the authors embraces learning experiences that vary widely in structure, student grouping, and time allotment. Primary emphasis is on exploration—the discovery of one's interests and capabilities—a long-standing and widely recognized goal of education for the middle school years.

All rapidly growing boys and girls need a health and physical education program that meets their needs for body building, social and recreational skills, self-understanding, and a moderate amount of competitive athletics. Required experiences in art, music, homemaking, and industrial arts also serve the cause of exploration and enrichment, especially when offered as "unified" or "related" arts.

Further enrichment may be provided by means of a variety of electives, minicourses, clubs, activities, and independent study opportunities. In these the main focus is often on the process, rather than the product, with student involvement being stressed. Many different ways of scheduling and staffing this portion of the curriculum may be found in junior high/middle schools today.

As young people and adults of similar interests work together in relatively informal situations, many of the goals of middle school education may be achieved. The variable component of the curriculum fulfills a vital role.

References

1. Sam E. James, "New Needs and a New Health Education Program for the Middle School," *Middle School Journal*, vol. 8, no. 1 (February, 1977), pp. 6–7, 16.
2. Charles E. Bucher, "A New Athletics Program for Our Schools," *NASSP Bulletin*, vol. 50, no. 309 (April, 1966), pp. 198–218; Paul Dreiske, "Are Organized Sports Child's Play?" *Family Safety*, vol. 32, no. 4 (Winter, 1973–74), pp. 19–20.
3. Conrad F. Toepfer, Jr., "Intramural and Interscholastic Athletics: Priori-

ties for the Middle Grades," *Dissemination Services on the Middle Grades*, vol. 4, no. 8 (May, 1973), pp. 1–4.

4. Richard Monte, "An Athletic Program with Opportunity for All," *Middle School Journal*, vol. 4, no. 2 (Summer, 1973), pp. 25–27.

5. Julian W. Smith, Reynold E. Carlson, George W. Donaldson, and Hugh B. Masters. *Outdoor Education*. 2d ed., (Englewood Cliffs, New Jersey: Prentice-Hall, 1972), p. 20.

6. Mary Louise Zieger, "Administering an Exploratory Program—A Working Plan." *Middle School Journal*, (Summer, 1973), pp. 17–22.

7. "Unified Arts of Wilbur Wright Middle School Offers 70 Mini-Courses." *Junior High/Middle School Bulletin*, Indiana State University, (Spring, 1974), pp. 1 and 3.

8. Richard W. Meister, "What About 'Unified Arts' in the Middle School?" *Educational Leadership*, (December, 1973), pp. 233–235.

9. William M. Alexander, Vynce A. Hines, and Associates, *Independent Study in Secondary Schools*, (New York: Holt, Rinehart, and Winston, 1967), p. 12.

10. Ronald W. Tyrrell, "Personalizing Educational Activities: An Approach to Student Directed Learning." *Middle School Journal*, (Spring, 1973), pp. 7–11.

11. William A. Cuff, "Do Middle and Junior High Schools Need Student Councils?" *Middle School Journal*, (Fall, 1974), p. 42.

12. *Ibid.*, p. 42.

13. See Carl F. Vaupel, "The Wonderful World of the Mini-Course Program," *Middle School Journal*, vol. VII, no. 2 (June, 1976), pp. 6–7; and John Frank, Jr., *Complete Guide to Co-Curricular Programs and Activities for the Middle Grades*, (West Nyack, New York; Parker, 1976), chapter 9.

14. For further information, see William Van Til, Gordon F. Vars, and John H. Lounsbury, *Modern Education for the Junior High School Years*, 2d ed., (Indianapolis: Bobbs-Merrill), 1967, pp. 466–7.

8 EVALUATING AND REPORTING STUDENT PROGRESS

Ask a middle school student how he determines what his teachers really consider important in education, and he quite rightly points to the way they evaluate and report student progress. In too many schools, a noble philosophy, a fine curriculum, and inspired teaching are consistently undermined by archaic, unscientific, and inhumane evaluation and reporting procedures. Any attempt to improve education for the middle school years must also include careful scrutiny of this vital phase of the educational process.

There is no intent here to replicate the advice to be found in standard textbooks on measurement and evaluation. No doubt there is much room for improvement in the way most teachers evaluate student progress. Large classes and heavy teaching loads make it difficult for teachers to follow the procedures that they know are recommended by measurement experts. Nor do we intend to rehash all the arguments about grading and reporting student progress, so aptly summarized by Terwillinger,[1] Bellanca,[2] Simon and Bellanca,[3] and by Kirschenbaum, Simon, and Napier.[4] Instead, we wish to focus on a few fundamental issues particularly pertinent to evaluating and reporting student progress during the middle school years.

Evaluation

Consider, for example, the fundamental question of what standard of comparison will be used in evaluation. What does the word "Good!" mean at the top of a student's paper? Does it mean good in comparison with others in the class, good use of his ability regardless of what others did, or good improvement over his previous paper? Too often a teacher's evaluation is a mixture of all three, further garbling the message. Most letter marking systems are even more confusing, since personality factors such as classroom behavior have a way of influencing the grade. Meaningful evaluation must clearly designate the standard of comparison being used and not mix data based on different standards. Let us look at the four major alternatives.

Normative evaluation

By far the most prevalent approach is to compare a student's performance with that of other students. The normative group may consist of others in the same class, all students of a similar age or grade level in the school, or samples drawn from throughout the school district, the state, or the nation. This is essentially a competitive system, in which, by its very nature, some students will be "average," some "above average," and some "below average." Grading on the curve is one of the more notorious instances of this approach, a procedure widely damned but even more widely practiced at all levels of the education system.

Defenders of normative evaluation say that students should get used to "dog-eat-dog" competition because "that's life." They overlook the fact that adults usually can choose with whom they will compete, whereas students have no choice whatsoever in required courses, and only limited options in most elective programs. Moreover, adults are seldom evaluated with the stringency applied to school students. A supervisor might be able to rate all the secretaries within a given jurisdiction on a scale from A to F, but such ratings, even if made, seldom become public knowledge, and most offices can find useful employment even for those on the lower end of the distribution. In other words, in life, evaluation resembles "pass-fail" more than "curve grading."

Even if real life were more competitive than it is at present, this does not necessarily mean that identical pressures should be imposed on growing children. One function of the school is to protect a young person from the rigors of real life until he has the maturity, skills, and knowledge to meet them with reasonable assurance of success.

Students who are consistently rated at the low end of the distribution are bound to conclude that they are of little worth, "stupid," or "dumb." Likewise, students who surpass their peers time after time almost inevitably conclude that they are better than others. As damaging as this self-stereotyping may be, there is an added delusion based on differences among comparison groups. The poorest student in a select group of extremely capable young people may come to think of himself as not very bright, whereas the best student in a class of slow learners may overestimate his capabilities. In short, competitive evaluation may lead to grossly distorted self-concepts, especially for those on either end of the distribution. These effects are particularly damaging during the middle school years, a time when most young people are already going through an identity crisis.

Although normative evaluation has many harmful effects when used as the exclusive or even the dominant basis of comparison, we are not advocating that it be completely abolished. Students want to know how their work compares with others, and parents have a right to know how their child's work compares with state or national norms. This information, provided on occasion and placed within the context of evaluation based on other standards, can help a student and his parents to arrive at a more realistic assessment of both progress and potential.

Reporting a student's performance as compared with classmates is optional for teachers in the Kent State University Middle School, Kent, Ohio.[5] If they choose to do this, they must use either a standard form of histogram, which divides class performance into no more than five levels, or a verbal description, such as "top third" or "below the median." This reminds teachers that even the best of measurements is only approximate in education, and it spares them the many hair-splitting arguments that often arise when teachers presume to grade students with the precision implied by symbols such as "C+" or "B—." Standardized test data based on state and national norms are interpreted to students and their parents in this school at least once during the middle school years. This information is especially useful in career planning.

Normative evaluation does have a role in a total evaluation and reporting system, but the comparison group must be clearly designated, the rating intervals no more precise than warranted, and this should not be the primary basis on which student performance is judged.

Criterion-referenced evaluation

The education profession is going through a resurgence of interest in behavioral objectives, accountability, and performance-based evaluation. Performance in this case is evaluated in relation to some specified standard or criterion, not in comparison to the performance of other students. Indeed, a standard of performance is an essential element of behavioral objectives. For example, an objective in a physical education unit on basketball might be stated as follows: The student will sink eight out of ten free throws. A student who cannot do this at the conclusion of the unit has failed, regardless of what the other students can do.

In a less precise form, criterion-referenced evaluation has been with us for a long time in the guise of "grade level standards." Many teachers carry with them an image of what an "average" seventh grader "ought" to be able to do. Consciously or unconsciuosly this standard may be applied to all seventh graders, regardless of individual background or ability. Unfortunately, these standards are seldom spelled out precisely nor are they made public for the scrutiny of either students or parents. Moreover, teachers vary widely in the standards they apply, and their individual standards may be unduly influenced by personal biases and prejudices.

Fundamental to this approach is the assumption that it is possible to establish criteria of performance that can be applied equally to all students. Since the hallmark of the middle school is student diversity, criterion-referenced evaluation may appear inappropriate. Yet, there are common skills and concepts that educators can identify as essential for all; these might well be spelled out in performance terms with established criteria. Since many of them are taught in elementary school, middle school educators might use criterion-referenced evaluation to diagnose the status of students in these fundamental learnings as a basis for prescribing remedial or developmental instruction.

The Continuous Progress component of the curriculum design proposed in this book focuses on competence in reading, certain mathematical skills and concepts, and foreign language skills (for those who elect this subject). Other skills, such as problem solving, value clarification, and group processes are emphasized in the core component. The latter are much more difficult to specify in precise terms, so criteria must of necessity be more general. School personnel should very carefully scrutinize the body of skills and concepts they propose as absolutely essential for all students. Otherwise, anything and everything may be tagged with the essential label, allowing too little school time for individualization.

Criterion-referenced evaluation may also be applied to goals set by the student under teacher guidance. This approach is most commonly found in independent study and contract grading. Note that here the student chooses whether or not he wishes to become involved in determining criteria and working toward them. Such an approach not only allows for individual differences but helps students to discover their own potentialities and to learn how to organize their efforts to achieve an objective.

Symbols can be a problem in criterion-referenced evaluation. Technically, any performance below the criterion level is a "failure." Yet a student who consistently sinks seven out of ten foul shots could hardly be considered a failure in shooting baskets. A,B,C, marks are misleading here, because they usually connote performance compared with a norm group. We have already alluded to the hazards of comparing a student to some arbitrary and mythical "average 8th grader" or "typical A student." Percentages can also be misleading. A student who meets the criterion by sinking eight out of ten free throws has achieved 100% of the criterion, but certainly is not sinking 100% of his throws. Perhaps the best solution is to avoid symbols altogether and simply report the criterion set and the performance actually achieved. Whether sinking an average of seven out of ten free throws is "good," or "bad" involves value judgments that are not part of the criterion-referenced evaluation process, but instead involve considerations of student ability and effort.

Effort evaluation

Teachers expect students to work hard, and some kind of effort rating may be found on many progress reports. Such an evaluation must be based on some estimate of student ability—what he could do if he "really tried." For example, the following rating scale is applied to students in Harmon Middle School, Aurora, Ohio.

ACHIEVEMENT IN RELATION TO ABILITY

(+) Working at or near capacity
(S) Making moderate use of ability
(N) Working substantially below ability

Each student should be evaluated strictly on his own performance and ability, without reference to external criteria or to reference groups. This approach to evaluation is thus highly personal and individualized, a characteristic much needed in evaluating such a heterogeneous population as middle school students. Since each student is pitted against himself, a less capable student who does his best is rewarded with a high rating, encouraging him to continue to strive. Conversely, the bright student who loafs receives a low rating, which may spur him to greater effort. Effort evaluation is advocated as a means of providing for individual differences and motivating all students to do their best at all times. By rewarding effort, it helps students to understand that their personal worth is not solely dependent upon how they rank academically with their peers.

A drawback of this approach is the difficulty in obtaining a reliable estimate of a student's ability. Standardized test results can be of some help, and cumulative records can give the teacher some idea of previous performance. After working with the student in the classroom for a while, the teacher can also observe how well the student does when he appears to be "turned on" by a project or topic. The best a teacher can do is to combine all these clues and still make ample allowance for error. Student self-evaluations and frequent feedback from parents help to verify the teacher's judgment. Since ability estimates are crude at best, teachers should probably not be expected to judge a student's effort level much more precisely than in the example above.

Progress evaluation

Normative, criterion-referenced, and effort evaluations all attempt to measure student performance at a given point. These "snapshots" of student performance reveal progress only when compared with similar "snapshots" taken at an earlier time.

Here we are concerned with a type of evaluation that measures change over time and uses the change itself, not the level of performance, as the basis for evaluation. Consider, for example, two students who read 185 words per minute with 95% comprehension. If after six weeks of instruction Student A now reads 200 words per minute with the same comprehension, and Student B now reads 225 words per minute, Student B has made greater progress or growth over time.

Teachers are admonished to take students where they are and to help them progress as far as they can. Consequently, it is only natural to consider progress or growth as a basis for student evaluation. As in ability evaluation, the student is competing with himself, trying to exceed his previous record. Progress evaluation might appear to have the same individualization and motivation advantages as effort rating, without the difficulties in judging ability.

The problem in this approach to evaluation lies in determining what is good progress. Test makers often warn of the "topping out" effect; that is, students who are already performing well have relatively little room for improvement, whereas students at the other end of the scale can show considerable gain with relatively little effort. Hence, any arbitrary scale applied in measuring progress would handicap the good student and unfairly reward the less capable.

Consider the two reading students, for example. If both students have equal ability and have the potential to read 250 words per minute, it will be harder for Student B to increase his rate from 225 to 250 that for Student A to increase from 200 to 225. Yet the gain expected is the same in both cases. If progress evaluation is the dominant approach, students may try to beat the system by deliberately doing poorly on entry level exams or projects, so that they can register larger gains later on.

It is clear from the above discussion that there are advantages and disadvantages in applying each of the bases for evaluation; hence, no one approach should be used exclusively. Both written and oral evaluations of a student's work should indicate the standard being applied: "Mary, that was a good oral report because you met nearly all of the criteria we agreed on," not "That was a good oral report, Mary;" "This composition is not as well done as some of your previous work," not "This is a poor composition."

Student self-evaluation

Since the major goal of evaluation is to help the student determine his status in order to chart further learning, he should be involved at every stage. He should participate in setting goals and selecting objectives, determining the means used to achieve them, and selecting the procedures to be used in evaluating progress. Whatever the basis of comparison, student estimates and judgments should play an integral role. Students need to learn which standard is most appropriate for the particular kinds of learnings being evaluated. Where student self-ratings differ markedly from the teacher's, a conference can be informative for both parties. The student may be helped to see more clearly the meaning of the standards being applied, and the teacher may learn about student efforts which had not been obvious. Even more important, the student is helped to learn the difficult but extremely important skills of self-evaluation.

A strong case for student self-evaluation was made many years ago by a committee of the Metropolitan Detroit Bureau of Cooperative School Studies. As they put it, "the student's *own* interpretation of the meaning and value of what he does in the classroom is highly significant for his learning and for his development as a person. In the last analysis, each person has to learn 'on his own.' "[6]

Reporting

Mixing evaluations based on different kinds of standards is especially hazardous in reporting to parents. The dual marking system is a step in the right direction, in which one set of symbols is used to indicate performance compared with classmates and a different set to indicate effort. The junior high school in Wooster, Ohio, uses three sets: A—F to indicate achievement (class comparison); 1,2,3 to indicate effort (comparison with own ability); and S,N and U to rate citizenship (satisfactory, needs improvement, unsatisfactory).

Progress through a nongraded program may be indicated by means of a graph. The graph can be printed out as a line of asterisks by a data processing machine, or, as in Pike County, Georgia, teachers can X in the proper block on a graph 27 spaces high. Evidence of growth may be presented by marking the student's proficiency level at both the beginning and the end of the marking period. If the levels are defined in terms of specified criteria, the graph may communicate both criterion-referenced evaluation and growth over time.

Most progress reports include some comments on the student's personal-social adjustment. Checklists include such items as the following, taken from the East Lansing, Michigan, Middle School Progress Report. A (+) before the item indicates especially positive behavior, a (−) indicates that improvement is needed, and no mark recorded means that the student is performing satisfactorily.

Is attentive.
Follows directions.
Brings necessary materials to class.
Makes use of class time.
Contributes in class.
Is courteous; respects rights of others.

A desirable feature of this checklist is the provision for both positive and negative feedback on student behavior. Too often such checklists report only misbehavior. Information of a negative nature might best be communicated through a personal conference.

Since any set of symbols or checklist statements is impersonal and subject to misinterpretation, there should be ample space on any report form for written comments by both teacher and student.

With the availability of inexpensive photocopying machines, it is feasible to make progress reporting even more personalized. Each teacher can make up an individual form, explaining in general terms what the class has been doing, but allowing space for comments, ratings, or other information about each individual child. The task

is to establish enough school-wide uniformity of procedure to minimize confusion and simplify record keeping, while at the same time
enabling teachers to communiçate as precisely as possible how they
evaluate students.

The issue of uniformity *versus* individualism arises again in
scheduling student progress reports. Ideally, teachers should report
at the conclusion of major units of work, regardless of where that
event falls on the calendar. On the other hand, parents are accustomed
to receiving progress reports at regular intervals, usually every six
or nine weeks. The compromise utilized in one middle school is to
authorize teachers to send home reports whenever they deem it
appropriate, but *at least* once each quarter.

Regardless of frequency and format, no written report can take
the place of face-to-face communication. This is especially true when
dealing with objectives in the affective domain—attitudes, apprecia-
tions, and values. Teachers should frequently confer with students,
with parents, and sometimes with both simultaneously. This, of course,
takes time and thoughtful preparation, but few educational activities
are more vital. Released time for parent conferences is provided for
many elementary teachers. It is even more important at the middle
school level, where parent-child communication often breaks down
and the stresses and strains of transescence demand cooperative help
and understanding from all the adults in a young person's life.

Since a major purpose of a reporting system is to communicate
with parents, they should be consulted when the system is being
evaluated or revised. This is not to say that parents should exercise
veto power over professional educators. Too often school people
excuse their failure to improve their marking and reporting system by
assuming that parents will not accept any change, usually on the basis
of comments by a few vocal individuals. Of course parents prefer a
system with which they are familiar, but they will accept changes that
can be shown to benefit students and still provide an accurate picture
of a child's school performance.

For example, Plainwell Middle School in Plainwell, Michigan,
reports a student's progress, effort, performance level, and personal-
social adjustment by means of the form shown in Figure 5. If parents
are still not satisfied, they may request letter grades. In a recent year,
only about 10 percent of them did so.

A parent advisory group, P.T.A. executive committee, or other
broadly based group may serve as a sounding board for any proposed
changes. Periodic questionnaires to parents, students, and teachers can
gain valuable feedback from all involved parties.[7] Final decisions must
be made by the professional educators, of course, but acceptance will
be enhanced if everyone concerned has had an opportunity for input.

Figure 5   Progress Report, Plainwell Middle School

Student's Name	Subject	Teacher	Grade	School Year
			6 7	1976-1977

Reporting Period   PROGRESS

1st   3rd
□ □ □ □   Your child has satisfactorily achieved all the objectives set for him/her this reporting period.
2nd   4th
□ □ □ □   Your child has satisfactorily achieved most of the objectives set for him/her this reporting period.

□ □ □ □   Your child has not satisfactorily achieved a significant portion of the objectives set for him/her this reporting period.

EFFORT

□ □ □ □   Is satisfactory

□ □ □ □   Is below expectation

WRITTEN COMMENTS

1st Report—Your child is working at Level___and is at/above/below grade level. Your child was absent___days this 9 weeks.

□   If this box is checked we are requesting a conference with you. Please call us.

2nd Report—Your child is working at Level___and is at/above/below grade level. Your child was absent___days this 9 weeks.

□   If this box is checked we are requesting a conference with you. Please call us.

3rd Report—Your child is working at Level___and is at/above/below grade level. Your child was absent___days this 9 weeks.

□   If this box is checked we are requesting a conference with you. Please call us.

4th Report—Your child is working at Level___and is at/above/below grade level. Your child was absent___days this 9 weeks.

□   If this box is checked we are requesting a conference with you. Please call us.

OTHER CONSIDERATIONS

A "√" means the student needs to make some improvement. An empty box means the student is performing satisfactorily.

Reporting Period

1st	2nd	3rd	4th	
□	□	□	□	Follows directions
□	□	□	□	Brings necessary materials to class
□	□	□	□	Uses class time effectively
□	□	□	□	Completes assignments on time
□	□	□	□	Cooperates in group work
□	□	□	□	Shows acceptable level of independence
□	□	□	□	Respects personal and school property
□	□	□	□	Takes part in class
□	□	□	□	Uses self–control
□	□	□	□	Is courteous and respects the rights of others
□	□	□	□	Is punctual
□	□	□	□	Exhibits a positive attitude toward school
□	□	□	□	Obeys school/ped rules

SUMMARY

Since variability characterizes both the student body and the curriculum we recommend for the middle school years, a similar diversity should mark the student evaluation and reporting procedures used. Normative evaluation should be used only where appropriate, mainly as a guidance device to let students know where they stand with reference to others. Criterion-referenced evaluation should be used where desired outcomes can be specified precisely, either by the staff or by the students, under teacher guidance. Effort ratings should be used to encourage students to make optimum use of their abilities, and evaluation of progress over time to help students learn to pace themselves. Student self-evaluation is essential, regardless of the standard of comparison being applied.

Reporting procedures should clearly indicate which standard of comparison is being applied, without mixing them. Written reports should encourage both teachers and students to add personal comments, and face-to-face conferences should be used to supplement the written word. Feedback from students, teachers, and parents should be solicited at regular intervals to identify any improvements needed in the evaluation and reporting system.

A process as complex as education cannot be evaluated or reported by simplistic means. Middle school educators should make full use of modern technology to communicate the marvelous intricacies of student growth and learning as clearly as possible.

References

1. James S. Terwilliger, *Assigning Grades to Students,* (Glenview, Illinois: Scott, Foresman, 1971).
2. James A. Bellanca, *Grading,* Professional Studies Series, (Washington: National Education Association, 1977).
3. Sidney B. Simon and James A. Bellanca, eds., *Degrading the Grading Myths: A Primer of Alternatives to Grades and Marks,* (Washington: Association for Supervision and Curriculum Development, 1976).
4. Howard Kirschenbaum, Sidney Simon, and Rodney W. Napier, *Wad-Ja-Get? The Grading Game in American Education,* (New York: Hart, 1971).
5. Gordon F. Vars, "Student Evaluation: A Design for the Middle School," *Clearing House,* vol. 45, no. 1 (September 1970), pp. 18–21.
6. *Pupil Self-Evaluation in the Classroom* (Detroit: Metropolitan Detroit Bureau of Cooperative School Studies, 1957), p. 26.
7. Gordon F. Vars, "Student Evaluation in the Middle School: A Second Report," *Clearing House,* vol. 49, no. 6 (February, 1976), pp. 244–245.

9
CURRICULUM
LEADERSHIP

The middle school curriculum needed by today's transescents is neither so complicated nor so expensive as to be out of the reach of any school. Moreover, the three major proposed curriculum components and their subdivisions all exist in some form in many places. However, to attain this curriculum, or a variation of it, calls for planning, patience, and considerable effort.

How then does one develop the type of teacher discussed in Chapter 1, and how do such teachers, together with administrators, bring the proposed curriculum into being? Though no single optimum answer exists, many general approaches, practices, and methods are known and can be brought to bear in appropriate combinations. It may be difficult to change the curriculum, but by no means is it impossible. Much more is now known about how learning takes place, how to modify behavior, who should be involved, what has worked and has not worked. Better materials, resources, and expertise are available to assist efforts at change.

Curriculum development is a major field in education which

warrants more attention than is possible here. However, a general consideration of curriculum leadership is in order, particularly as it relates to the model we propose. Some useful books on curriculum development are listed with the Resources for Middle School Educators at the end of this book.

Basic principles of curriculum change

Changing people

The fundamental premise that underlies the process of changing the curriculum, as we see it, has been known for a long time. It has been restated in various ways by different people during the last several decades but was perhaps best expressed by Alice Miel in the 1940s. Her doctoral dissertation on changing the curriculum was subsequently digested into a brief book.[1] She also condensed her ideas into a three-page article that was submitted for publication. The magazine editor subsequently telephoned her and said, "You have done a good job, but the editors are lazy people, so would you boil down into a single title all that you have written in your dissertation, condensed in your book and excerpted into the article—six or seven words that summarize everything you know about changing curriculum?" This seemed an impossible task, but she agreed to try. A few days later she called the editor and triumphantly gave him the title, "*Changing the Curriculum Means Changing People.*"[2]

Alice Miel was so right when she enunciated that principle many years ago. Unfortunately, her valuable advice has been largely ignored and hundreds of thousands of dollars have, for all practical purposes, been wasted on curriculum revision efforts that did not take this axiom into account. Leaders have tried to bypass the time-consuming and sometimes frustrating processes that involve people. They have concentrated instead on the more manageable things: hardware, materials, and the organizational aspects of curriculum. Had one tenth of the money spent on improving education been channelled towards research in methods of bringing about change in people, much more would have been accomplished at a considerable financial saving.

A corollary of the idea that changing the curriculum means changing people is the premise that *the classroom teacher is the ultimate curriculum-change agent.* All curriculum improvement efforts are essentially in-service education efforts directed toward improving teaching. No matter how extensive the curriculum planning or faculty self-study, the payoff is in what occurs during the interaction of students and teachers in the classroom. Curriculum development should seek to improve individual human beings, to make it possible for teachers to make more effective curriculum decisions as they interact with young people. Any other approach to curriculum development is likely to lead up a blind alley.

Too often our best plans and exciting new curriculum guides, though sincerely and conscientiously developed by groups, have little or no effect on the actual learning experiences that young people engage in during school. The late Kimball Wiles clearly stated this reality of curriculum planning when he wrote, "The real curriculum is the one the pupil experiences. Actually the expectations of curriculum designers may be illusions and the teachers' guides and syllabi mere paper representatives of hollow hopes."[3] So we must recognize and conscientiously take into account the enduring significance of the classroom teacher as the agent of curriculum change.

If changing the curriculum means changing the classroom teacher, the question is, how do you change people? The cynic would answer, "Slowly, if at all." We would say, "Slowly, but surely."

A first step is to realize that in one sense the word "change" is misleading. We do not believe that teachers have to be "changed" from bad to good, from wrong to right; for, as we see it, teachers are better prepared and have a better grasp of effective practices and sound philosophy than their performance might indicate. They need to be "released," rather than "changed," to be their best selves. In this connotation teachers really want to change. Given adequate support and encouragement, they can be more nearly the teachers they want to be. The "system," with its built-in expectations and restrictions, heavy responsibilities, and the need for survival, combine to counteract preparation and squelch idealism. All too soon, able young teachers become discouraged veterans who readily acknowledge that their performance is not fully justified, not optimal, nor even very effective, but who have accepted the apparent need to teach by a second-rate standard.

We believe the middle school is the best place in which to turn this situation around. Here desirable and significant changes can be made so that schools are a joy to both pupils and teachers, while truly meeting the needs of youth and the reasonable expectations of society. Inspired by being a part of a major educational movement, free from most stultifying traditions, encouraged by the eager, open early adolescents themselves, and supported by the growing body of educational philosophy and psychology that urges individualization and humanization, the middle school teacher can really be changed or freed, and can make a difference. Our society's condition practically makes such an effort mandatory, our professional stature demands that we try, and our personal goals should remain equally lofty.

Guidelines for curriculum improvement

While changing or altering people and their practices is not easy, there are enough general principles and specific techniques available to make efforts successful. We offer the following nine general principles as guidelines for curriculum improvement efforts:

1. Provide for the direct and full participation of the faculty in the efforts.
2. Provide leadership that is fully supportive, enthusiastic, and knowledgeable.
3. Provide time and resources for dealing with substantive curriculum improvement matters.
4. Provide for open two-way communications among all interested parties.
5. Provide "handles"—specific activities and methods for getting at curriculum problems and securing data and opinions for analysis and action.
6. Provide encouragement for experimentation and trial without pressure to succeed.
7. Provide for collegial support and cooperative effort.
8. Provide for ways of securing student input and keeping student needs central to the process of curriculum improvement.
9. Provide for parent and community involvement throughout.

In the remainder of this chapter a number of specific suggestions will be offered that reflect these general principles.

Group roles in curriculum improvement

The role of administrators

As the acknowledged educational leader in each school unit, the principal is the key to curriculum improvement. This certainly does not mean that he or she must make all of the decisions, but leadership from the front office is essential if teachers and other staff are to fulfill their roles in curriculum planning and development.

To call for administrators to become active in curriculum improvement is to call for something of a return to an earlier set of priorities. In recent years the managerial functions of administrators seem to have taken precedence over instructional functions. And the instructional leadership role to which the principal should return may not be identical to that of previous years.

Educational leadership still calls for sincere commitment to objectives. But in addition, it has come to demand a deep understanding of people, facility in handling human relationships, and a sense of timing. Decisions, such as when to take the initiative, when to wait, when to compromise, and when to adhere tenaciously to a principle are more matters of "feeling" than of "directing." The ability to perceive others' perceptions has little relationships to authority.

The indirect approach to curriculum development is often more productive than the direct approach. Rather than concentrating on the implementation of a "plan" to achieve a particular curriculum change, the "leader" might well be concerned primarily with developing a more supportive climate. People tend to perform at the level which is consistently expected of them. Sincerely requesting teachers' opinions, respecting their judgments, and demonstrating faith in people will move a faculty further along in curriculum development than a raft of memoranda and meetings.

Only as the working environment becomes conducive to growth will needed experimentation take place. The principal, more than anyone else, determines the climate of the school. By demonstrating respect for the ability of others, evidenced in the delegation of responsibility and support in its implementation, the principal sets the tone. By his own use of time and what it reveals about his priority of values—by putting people before paper—the principal contributes substantially to the atmosphere of the school. Taking a teacher's class to free that teacher for a curriculum-improvement activity or using administrative know-how to free groups of teachers for during-the-day curriculum work communicates a great deal. Accepting full responsibility for a miniclass "says" even more.

The educational leader can demonstrate greater approval to those who are experimental and less to those who prefer the status quo. (The reverse, of course, is usually the prevailing condition.)

Administrators can probably help more by questions asked than by answers given. They can insure that a full analysis of the current situation is made and that the implications of proposed alternatives are examined through thoughtful questions. They can remind the staff of agreed-upon objectives lest they be forgotten in nuts and bolts discussions. They can remind faculty of the need to involve everyone in the planning and projections. Sensitive leaders can make sure that evaluation and assessment procedures are built in as a part of the curriculum plan. Administrators, anxious to be curriculum engineers and leaders, must sometimes subordinate the executive or hierarchial role, while fully maintaining the posture of a professional teacher and emphasizing peer or collegial relationship.

The supportive climate sought is the culmination of hundreds of little things rather than the result of any major or dramatic action.

The principal who sincerely seeks to live by the maxim, "That which is instructionally desirable should administratively be made possible," will be able to offer leadership in changing the curriculum.

The principal should seek to understand the teachers better as individuals. As teachers are supposed to help students know themselves and feel good about themselves, so the principal should help faculty members come to grips with themselves as total human beings. Teachers, too, are engaged in the process of becoming. They sometimes need assistance in dealing with their own feelings and the feelings of others. This may be done by sponsoring a weekend retreat for a values clarification workshop, conducting a series of human relationship activities at faculty meetings, arranging for a resource person to work with the faculty over a period of time, or some combination of the above.

The particular curriculum development processes employed should reflect the kind of school desired. A humane middle school cannot be created through dictatorial, arbitrary curriculum development processes. That is, one does not employ one set of principles with the staff while trying to get them to operate by a different set in dealing with students. As Marshall McLuhan has taught us, "The medium is the message."

Over the years the authors have regularly and consistently heard the common complaint of the in-service teacher, "My principal won't let me try anything new." Although sometimes a rationalization for doing nothing, this complaint suggests that administrators should adopt as another maxim the Latin phrase, "*ne sim obex*"—simply translated, "May I not be an obstacle." So often administrators are cast in the role of being obstacles, guardians of the status quo. Even without overt intention, schools assume a domestication role and seem to value compliance and routine. A fundamental role of administrators desiring to encourage curriculum improvement is to open up and alter the protective, closed atmosphere that seems to reside in many schools.

The role of teachers

While administrators have a clear and special responsibility to serve as change agents, only when each individual faculty member sees himself in a similar capacity will enduring change occur.

One of the real handicaps to the improvement of education in America has been the industrial model of "boss and workers" that was applied to education early, has persisted in the minds of both teachers and the general public, and has recently been reinforced by the trend toward collective bargaining. However, in theory a school is made up of professional colleagues, one or two of whom have special service responsibilities to free the others to practice their profession more effectively. The medical model, as in a hospital, is perhaps a preferable prototype to emulate rather than the factory model, though implementation may be difficult.

Teachers have all too rarely seen themselves as independent, responsible, fully professional practitioners, yet in most American school systems they are or could be. Teachers usually have far more latitude and responsibility for deciding what to teach and how to teach than they seek to exercise. Blaming the textbook, the State Department, the supervisor, the administrator, are usually rationalizations rather than reasons for inactivity. The human inclination to lethargy, to opt for security, is often a greater detriment to improved practices than either the restrictive dictates of authorities or working conditions. As the funny paper philosopher, Pogo, sagely, if ungrammatically, put it, "We has met the enemy and he is us." Leadership for curriculum improvement can and should emerge from the faculty.

Individual teachers will want to seek the support and cooperation of other teachers. Often a single "pairing" will lead to changes that neither one could have achieved alone; for as misery loves company, so do change agents. The teachers who occupy the same pod or wing of a building, or who work on an interdisciplinary team, are natural allies and can be mutually supportive in planning and conducting innovations. Where such a team shares a planning period, an especially excellent basis for experimentation exists and should be exploited.

The way teachers talk about curriculum changes to students, parents, and community members also makes a difference. It is perfectly natural for teachers to have reservations about curriculum proposals with which they are not familiar. As professionals, however, they must be willing to study the evidence, express any doubts they have, and then give the new approach a fair trial if the consensus of the staff favors it. Change always demands extra time and energy, but the professional teacher willingly accepts a reasonable amount as the price of improving education for young people. Unfortunately, some teachers air their complaints to students, parents, and community members who are not in a direct position to act upon them, rather than working through the system, including their professional associations, to get their views heard.

The role of students and parents

Middle school youngsters or their parents are not as continuously and actively involved in curriculum improvement as teachers, but it would be a great mistake to assume that they have no role. Students are the *raison d'etre* of the institution itself. Their parents have more of a vested interest than any other group. Though one group is young and somewhat immature and the other is a "lay" group, they both can and should be brought into the curriculum improvement process. The initiative for their involvement lies necessarily with the faculty and administration.

Direct involvement of students in day-to-day curriculum planning is illustrated in the discussion of core curriculum in Chapter 5. Core students play a major role both in determining what is taught and how it is taught. But teacher-student planning should not be limited to the core. Student input is vital in all courses, subjects, and activities, even the highly structured sequential learning described in Chapter 6 on the continuous progress curriculum component.

Somewhat more formal means of soliciting student involvement may be needed in planning the overall school curriculum. For example, the student council or a special student advisory committee may assist the faculty in designing the exploratory and activities program described in Chapter 7. Interested students may even participate in committees revising school programs in the subject areas, such as science or health.

Questionnaire surveys of an entire student body may elicit many valuable suggestions and evaluations. As the direct consumers of the curriculum, students certainly are in the best position to make judgments. The *Student Opinion Inventory,* published in 1974 by the National Study of School Evaluation, is a very simple and inexpensive vehicle for securing the opinions of students in an organized, manageable way.[4]

Part A of the *Inventory* consists of 34 multiple choice items that assess students' attitudes toward school. The items can be grouped into subscales to give a separate reading on students' attitudes toward faculty, administrators, counselors, curriculum and instruction, cocurricular activities, and facilities. The items were thoroughly field-tested nationwide and the reliability and validity of the subscales were established.

Part B of the *Inventory* consists of twelve open-ended questions which solicit student recommendation about needed improvements.

Depending upon the size of the school and other factors, the entire student body or a random sample can be surveyed. Either way, the results will provide meaningful data for curriculum improvement efforts by a middle school faculty. Through both formal and informal means, students should be regularly and continuously consulted on what they view as important in education.

Parent involvement, although to a lesser degree, is also inherent in the curriculum proposed in this book. Parents may serve as resource people in regular courses and as consultants and advisors in the exploratory and enrichment program.

The Westchester Middle School of Chesterton, Indiana, has

developed a relatively formal and very successful program of community involvement in the instructional program. Citizens who contribute time and effort to the school's program are designated "Associate Faculty Members" and awarded an attractive certificate.[5]

Parent evaluation of the school curriculum should also be regularly solicited through parent-teacher organizations, parent-teacher conferences, lay advisory committees, and the countless informal contacts among people who share a common concern—the education of a particular group of students. An instrument for assessing parent opinion was published by the National Study of School Evaluation in 1977 as a companion to the *Student Opinion Inventory* mentioned above. The fifty-three item *Parent Opinion Inventory* seeks to assess parents' attitudes toward the school and its program, to provide parents an opportunity to make recommendations for improvement, and to provide data needed in making decisions. The instrument's low cost, ease of administration, and careful construction make the securing of substantial parent opinion readily achievable. Involvement of both parents and students is an essential part of the school self-study described later in this chapter, although either of these instruments may be used independently.

Curriculum improvement through in-service education

Throughout the nation a renewed emphasis on the in-service education of teachers has emerged. Several factors have contributed to this: (1) dissatisfaction with the degree of educational improvement achieved in the last twenty years; (2) the end of the student enrollment growth syndrome that has characterized and all but preoccupied public education since the close of World War II; (3) a reduction in the turnover rate of teachers which, with an increasing supply of teachers available, has encouraged greater attention to quality; (4) the increased willingness and readiness of institutions of higher education to move out into school settings and to cooperatively plan in-service educational experiences; and (5) the expanding interest of teachers in raising their level of performance.

Though summer study continues as a popular means for intensive in-service education, teachers increasingly anticipate and do participate in continuous programs of in-service education during the school year. In many states the term "staff development" has become the new label for in-service education during the school year. While the trend to provide more professional growth activities during the school year brings with it a variety of problems, it certainly increases the opportunities for teachers to engage in curriculum development. These opportunities should be fully utilized by middle school personnel.

Curriculum improvement must be a continuous, ongoing process. This can most likely be achieved when it is approached directly, not merged into a general program of staff development. Support and encouragement by the school system's central office staff is essential in marshalling the resources—the time, money, and personnel needed to deal with curriculum problems.

Needs assessment.   Many schools and school systems are applying a systems approach to in-service education. Plans are drawn up whereby a school faculty, usually through a steering committee and often with community assistance, makes a careful assessment of student needs. This involves examination of test data, interviews with students and graduates, as well as the use of other data-gathering techniques. The documented pupil needs then lead to the identification of teacher competencies and other materials and services necessary for meeting those needs. Experiences designed to develop the competencies become, in turn, the focus of the in-service education or staff development program. College courses tailored to achieve the competencies identified are often a part of the effort.

Self-study.   Another major activity that can lead to substantial curriculum improvement is a school self-study. Self-studies are a required part of the accreditation process for high schools in all the regional accrediting associations, and for middle schools in a few of the regions. Whether required for accreditation or not, self-study is an extremely valuable procedure. Normally the entire faculty is involved, all aspects of the school program are reviewed, and recommendations for improvement are enumerated. Some schools utilize the services of a consultant during the self-study.

Schools seeking accreditation normally expect a visiting committee upon completion of the self-study. Though the visiting committee reinforces the self-study process, it is not essential.

A nationally recognized handbook for conducting a self-study is *The Junior High School/Middle School Evaluative Criteria.*[6] This instrument, published by the National Study of School Evaluation, was developed by middle school and junior high school specialists and, following extensive field testing, was made available in 1970. A companion volume, *Elementary School Evaluative Criteria*, utilizes essentially the same format.

Shadow-study.   Another technique that can assist in a serious examination of a school's educational program is the shadow study.[7] This involves following a particular pupil through the entire school day, while making regular notes of the pupil's activities and environment. A series of such studies dramatically depict the school as it is from the student standpoint. Somehow the curriculum looks different when viewed this way.

Shadow studies may be conducted by student teachers, by central office personnel, and by administrators, as well as by teachers. No formal training is needed. Middle schools in the same locale might trade teams to conduct shadow studies for one another's schools. Several studies done in a middle school will yield much valuable data for discussion and analysis.

Intervisitation. Intervisitation is an older but still effective means of fostering curriculum improvement. Watching fellow teachers work in another setting is always a meaningful and satisfying activity for teachers. As one wise middle school principal put it, "If you see someone doing something better than you do, you can learn something new. If you find you are already doing it better than they are, you find further validation of the good things you are already doing." And "seeing yourself" in another teacher's performance may be as instructive as seeing what that teacher does.

Even more important, for most teachers, is the opportunity to watch the reactions of students to the curriculum or methods being employed. Although there are some apparent fallacies in this reasoning, most teachers feel that if the students respond with enthusiasm, the material and approach must be all right. No amount of data can substitute for the value of seeing students at work.

Sites for visits may be, but need not be, "model" middle schools or those with "innovative" programs. Sending a team of teachers to make the visit makes possible a more adequate survey of the complexities of the program observed. It also ensures that there will be colleagues who can provide support and encouragement while trying out some of the ideas acquired from the visit.

Study of the learners. A comprehensive and well-planned study of the nature and needs of transescent learners is an especially important activity for a middle school seeking to improve its practices. Such a study could well include the use of resource persons—doctors, social workers, psychologists, community recreation personnel, policemen, parents, and the students themselves. This study would make use of standard professional literature. New data covering a range of factors such as achievement, interests, maturity, age, and family, can be secured to develop a meaningful profile of the current student body. The present curriculum can then be analyzed to see how well it correlates with the data secured.

Utilizing faculty meetings. Despite the negative feelings often evoked by the term, *faculty meeting*, such meetings can be helpful in curriculum improvement and professional growth experiences. A first step is to involve faculty members as major participants and to focus on real and truly professional matters. Reading announcements and dealing with "administrivia," while occasionally necessary, are insufficient justification for holding a faculty meeting.

One specific technique for improving these meetings is to turn a particular session, possibly one every month, into a "clinic." A teacher agrees in advance to present to his colleagues a particular real curricular problem with background information and details sufficient for thorough discussion. The faculty, serving as resource persons, suggest ways of dealing with the problem. It is best if some kind of consensus is reached on the most likely solution so that a clear direction for action emerges. The teacher, armed with this consensus and feeling the support of colleagues, is particularly motivated to try. Follow-up reports are helpful and usually well received, as the group has a stake in the matter.

At another time a faculty meeting might well be the occasion for a case conference. The teachers who work directly with a particular student would discuss his needs and problems, in front of the remainder of the faculty. The floor is then open for other staff members' suggestions.

Reports from various committees and the activities suggested in the foregoing section are also bases for professional faculty meetings. In these meetings the "tone" should be one of a collection of professional colleagues who have come together to share their expertise, rather than a meeting called by the administration to hear a report. Large faculties may need to subdivide into houses, grade level groups, teaching teams, or random groups to keep numbers small enough for genuine interaction.

Clarifying objectives. The end result of all efforts to change the curriculum through changing people is to modify their purposes, goals, and objectives. There is no shortcut to real and lasting improvement that bypasses hard and serious thinking about the objectives of education. Many would shun such effort, feeling it is more nearly an exercise for college education classes than something of value in the day-to-day instruction of transescents. Yet, *every* decision made by a teacher or administrator reflects, consciously or subconsciously, that person's philosophy of education. Curriculum planning involves making choices, and making choices necessarily involves objectives and values. Only with a particular goal in mind can an educator determine whether one topic is preferable to another or one method more appropriate than another.

Ultimately, the curriculum is made in the classroom. Little significant change will take place if the teachers who control the minute-by-minute curriculum decisions do not seek to achieve the same objectives as those who planned the course of study, wrote the textbooks, or otherwise preplanned the curriculum. The objectives of the teacher, at a very practical level, must be altered if the real "take-home curriculum" is to be altered.

In order to assist in serious considerations of goals and objectives, a faculty might want to review some appropriate books. Bloom's and Krathwohl's taxonomies,[8] Gronlund's *Stating Behavioral Objectives for Classroom Instruction*,[9] and Combs' *Educational Accountability, Beyond Behavioral Objectives*[10] would be a few appropriate resources. The issues in humanism *vs.* behaviorism can be identified and debated. Some actual experiences in trying to write objectives in behavioral terms, particularly those in the affective domain, will sensitize teachers to the issues and cause them to think more deeply about objectives than they otherwise might.

Another way to elicit thought about objectives is for teachers to spell out on paper the procedures they follow in evaluating and marking student progress. After this has been done, they can analyze their statements to see what objectives are clearly reflected by their practices and which are seemingly ignored or contradicted. This activity might also be undertaken by teaching teams, grade level staffs, or other small groups.

In attempts to study the area of goals and objectives, a major point is to reduce the gap between the generally accepted, often glibly stated, but vague objectives to which we give lip service, and the almost subconscious but very real objectives that determine the in-process curriculum decisions which every teacher makes nearly every minute.

Implementing the curriculum proposed in this book

Thus far we have discussed general procedures for improving any middle school curriculum. Now we turn to a few specific suggestions for implementing the middle school curriculum design advocated in the book. Each of the recommended curriculum components presents specific implementation challenges, but "to be forewarned is to be forearmed."

The *core component* described in Chapter 5 probably departs most significantly from common middle school practice; hence it requires particular care in its implementation. On the other hand, more than twenty-five years ago Harold Alberty and some of his students made a number of recommendations for implementation that are still valid today.[11] Eight years later Lucile Lurry and Elsie Alberty wrote a book that details how a core program can be established in a large school system.[12] More recently, Robert Hanes has described the role of central office personnel in core program development,[13] and Ralph Chalender has discussed the critical role of the school principal.[14] The recommendations that follow incorporate the ideas of these and other pioneers of the core movement, as well as the experiences of the present writers.

Administrative commitment. Both research[15] and experience with core verify the key role of administrative leadership in implementing this or any other significant departure from conventional practice. The superintendent and the building principal must at least be willing to give the core program a fair chance for success by providing staff planning time, a modest outlay of money for staff development, and above all, psychological support. This commitment must extend over a reasonable period of time—perhaps three years. Too often innovations are abandoned just as they are beginning to bear fruit.

At the same time, administrators must take steps to reassure the board of education, parents, and the general public that student learning under the new program will at least equal the current level. Citing previous research on the effectiveness of block-time and core programs is helpful, but continuous and thorough evaluation must also be built into the plan of implementation. Despite its limitations, standardized testing in the basic skills should be carried out routinely in core classes, in addition to the more innovative evaluation procedures dictated by the nature of core.

Teacher philosophy. The prime requisite of a successful core teacher is a top priority commitment to helping young people deal with problems—both personal problems and those that impinge upon them from society at large. Teachers who already have this orientation or who are willing to give it a fair trial should be encouraged, but not required, to join the team that is to develop a core program. These staff members will then deal more specifically with the questions posed in Chapter 4.

Broken front approach to curriculum change. Although we believe that core is the best vehicle for achieving some of the goals of middle school education, it obviously is not the only one. Likewise, core teaching does not appeal to all teachers, even those in the subject areas that are absorbed or replaced by a particular core program. Therefore we suggest that core be developed as an alternative, perhaps paralleling an interdisciplinary team program and a conventional separate-subjects approach. Schools already organized on a house or school-within-a-school plan can implement this approach easily, with teachers, students, and parents exercising some choice among the alternatives available. Of course, staff members must keep their colleagues, the students, parents, and the community at large informed of what they are doing.

Curriculum design. Once the core staff members have been identified, they can begin to design the curriculum.[16] Careful study of the needs of contemporary transescents as they grow up in today's world should lead to identification of a set of problem areas or centers of experience. These, in turn, should be elaborated in resource units and other teaching aids.

Staff development. Parallel with curriculum development and, perhaps, even preceding it, attention should be focused on the methods that are especially crucial in core teaching, such as teacher-student planning, developing skills within a problem-centered unit, providing guidance in a classroom setting, etc.[17] The references cited in Chapter 5 give many practical "how-to" suggestions.

Student evaluation. Students will not engage fully in open-ended examination of problems if they know that their work will be marked in the traditional A–B–C manner. A more individualized, flexible system of evaluating and reporting is needed, as discussed in Chapter 8. Such a system must be initiated, at least for the core classes, at the time the core program is established. The hobgoblin of schoolwide consistency in marking must not be permitted to impose an evaluation system that contradicts the goals of a particular program.

The *continuous progress* component described in Chapter 6 also requires commitment and expenditure of time, effort, and money. If the school system cannot afford one of the commercially developed systems, such as the Westinghouse Corporation's PLAN, then a great deal of time must be set aside for the staff to develop their own nongraded curriculum and the instructional materials needed to implement it. Student accounting is also a serious problem in highly individualized programs. Teachers must know each child's exact status in each nongraded sequence. Without a computer, this too, takes endless hours of bookkeeping. Fortunately, some publishers are beginning to provide the necessary forms and charts. Ultimately, of course, the student must accept responsibility for monitoring his own performance.

Conventional marking systems are as inadequate for the continuous progress approach as they are for core, so staff members must tackle this problem as they develop the new curriculum. Checklists of competencies are used in some schools, and a few have even designed computer programs that print out a small bar graph indicating how far a student has progressed on a continuum of competencies.

The *exploration* and *activities* component touches the lives of every staff member, so total staff involvement is required, even though the program may be planned and coordinated by a small committee. Students, parents, and the community at large also have a role to play, as indicated in the guidelines suggested in Chapter 7. Keeping track of the many options available and maintaining a record of each student's participation imposes additional bookkeeping chores. Fortunately, most middle school students are mature enough to keep a continuous record of their participation in activities and other informal learning experiences.

SUMMARY

Improving the curriculum calls for leadership and involvement. The process is not easy; it requires understanding, skill, patience, and continuing effort. Fundamental to achieving lasting change are the twin propositions: (1) Changing the curriculum means changing people, and (2) The classroom teacher is the ultimate change agent. Only as teachers interact differently with students in the classroom will there be change in the curriculum that is actually experienced.

Teachers inherently desire to improve their effectiveness, and thus change efforts become largely efforts to assist, support, and encourage teachers in their own professional growth and development.

The administrator has a key role in establishing the climate needed for curriculum development. Personal example and sensitivity to people are all-important.

In addition, teachers need to exert leadership in curriculum improvement. They need to see themselves as change agents. Both as individuals and in cooperation with colleagues, teachers should experiment in efforts to provide more effective education.

Students, the ultimate consumers of the curriculum, have an important role to play in improvement efforts. Their input should be secured both as an on-going part of student-teacher planning in classes and through specific school-wide efforts to solicit it.

Ongoing in-service education programs and regular faculty meetings should be fully utilized as means of achieving curriculum improvement. Change is most likely to occur when a specific problem, activity, project, or program is the focus of the faculty's concern.

Implementing the middle school curriculum proposed in this book is not easy, but it can be done if educators work together to apply some of the specific suggestions detailed throughout this book. The challenge is to make education for the middle school years a vital force in achieving the lofty goals of American education in ways that reflect the unique characteristics and needs of this age group.

References

1. Alice Miel, Changing the Curriculum: A Social Process, (New York: Appleton-Century-Crofts, 1946).
2. This is an authentic anecdote. The editor was William Van Til, at that time editor of the Intercultural Education News.
3. Kimball Wiles in the Foreword to The Junior High School We Saw: One Day in the Eighth Grade, (Washington, D.C.: Association for Supervision and Curriculum Development, 1964), p. v.
4. Available from the National Study of School Evaluation, 1201 Arlington Blvd., Arlington, Virginia, 12201.
5. Don K. Deller and Jack E. Wright," An Associate Faculty Program Incorporates Community Resources," Middle School Journal, vol. VIII, no. 3 (August, 1977), p. 11.
6. Published by the National Study of School Evaluation, 1201 Arlington Blvd., Arlington, Virginia, 12201.
7. John H. Lounsbury and Jean V. Marani, The Junior High School We Saw: One Day in the Eighth Grade, (Washington, D.C.: Association for Supervision and Curriculum Development, 1964), 70 pp. See especially Chapter 5.
8. Benjamin S. Bloom, ed., Taxonomy of Educational Objectives, Handbook I: Cognitive Domain, (New York: David McKay, 1956), David R. Krathwohl and others, Taxonomy of Educational Objectives, Handbook II: Affective Domain, (New York: David McKay, 1964).
9. Norman E. Gronlund, Stating Behavioral Objectives for Classroom Instruction, (New York: Macmillan, 1970).
10. Arthur Combs, Educational Accountability, Beyond Behavioral Objectives, (Washington, D.C.: Association for Supervision and Curriculum Development, 1974).
11. Harold Alberty and others, "How to Develop a Core Program in the High School," (Columbus: College of Education, Ohio State University, 1949). (Mimeographed.)
12. Lucile L. Lurry and Elsie J. Alberty, Developing a High School Core Program, (New York: Macmillan, 1957).
13. Robert C. Hanes, "The Role of Central Office Personnel in Core Program Development," Common Learnings: Core and Interdisciplinary Team Approaches, ed. Gordon F. Vars (Scranton, Pennsylvania: Intext, 1969), pp. 161–169.
14. Ralph E. Chalender, "The Role of the Principal in Core Program Development," Common Learnings: Core and Interdisciplinary Team Approaches (Scranton, Pennsylvania: Intext, 1969), pp. 171–178.
15. Gordon F. Vars, "Administrative Leadership—Key to Core Program

Development," *Bulletin of the National Association of Secondary School Principals*, vol. 46 (February, 1962), pp. 91–103.

16. See: "Preplanning and Content Organization in a Core Program," *Modern Education for the Junior High School Years*, 2d ed., by William Van Til, Gordon F. Vars, and John H. Lounsbury, (Indianapolis: Bobbs-Merrill, 1967), pp. 259–281.

17. See: "Teaching Core," in *Modern Education for the Junior High School Years*, 2d ed., by William Van Til, Gordon F. Vars, and John H. Lounsbury, (Indianapolis: Bobbs-Merrill, 1967), pp. 283–314.

RESOURCES FOR MIDDLE SCHOOL EDUCATORS

The professional literature in middle school education is expanding rapidly. Educators who serve at this level need to be on the alert for new resources.

Periodical literature is a major and continuously current source of ideas. The *Middle School Journal*, a quarterly publication of the National Middle School Association, is obviously devoted exclusively to the intermediate level. It is available through an individual membership or by subscription. The organization also publishes a newsletter and occasional booklets and research reports. (P. O. Box 968, Fairborn, Ohio 45324). *Clearing House, Educational Leadership, The National Elementary Principal,* and the *Bulletin of the National Association of Secondary School Principals* are excellent periodicals which frequently include articles focusing on the middle school years. The Educational Leadership Institute, P. O. Box 863, Springfield, Massachusetts 01101, provides several services to those concerned with the emerging adolescent learner. These include an annual journal, *Transescence,* and

Dissemination Services on the Middle Grades, a monthly leaflet that describes promising practices in education for the middle school years.

Of special interest and value to middle school educators is the National Middle School Resource center, a federally funded ESEA Title IV–C project attached to the Indianapolis, Indiana, Public Schools (120 East Walnut Street). The Center maintains extensive files of relevant materials which can be circulated. Consultants are also available to conduct in-service sessions.

Many state associations publish newsletters, pamphlets, or annual booklets. The *Junior High/Middle School Bulletin,* edited by Max Bough and published three times a year by the School of Education, Indiana State University, Terre Haute, has been a major resource for long years. The National Association for Core Curriculum, 407D White Hall, Kent State University, Kent, Ohio, regularly publishes an informative newsletter, *The Core Teacher.* The Junior High School Association of Illinois has published a major study report annually. The 1976 volume, *Discipline in the Junior High/Middle School,* is available from The Interstate Printers and Publishers of Danville, Illinois.

The Association for Supervision and Curriculum Development has prepared a videotape for staff development, "Designing a Middle School for Early Adolescents." Featuring seven well-known educators, the program is available in ¾″ videocassettes or ½″ reel to reel. (1701 K Street, N. W., Suite 1100, Washington, D.C. 20036). "The Modern Middle School," a series of four filmstrip-cassette programs, is available from Teacher Education Resources, 2001 N. W. 58th Terrace, Gainesville, Florida.

Published books, available in school and college libraries, are a major source of information and thought for most intermediate educators. Listed below are a limited number of basic references, including some older, but still pertinent, volumes.

Selected References

Alexander, William, et al. *The Emergent Middle School.* 2d ed. New York: Holt, Rinehart, and Winston, 1969.

Bondi, Joseph. *Developing Middle Schools: A Guidebook.* New York: MSS Information Corporation, 1972.

Bough, Max E. and Hamm, Russell L., eds. *The American Intermediate School.* Danville, Illinois: The Interstate Printers and Publishers, 1974.

Curtis, Thomas E. and Bidwell, Wilma W. *Curriculum and Instruction for Emerging Adolescents.* Reading, Mass.: Addison-Wesley, 1977.

De Vita, Joseph C.; Pumerantz, Philip; and Wilklow, Leighton B. *The Effective Middle School.* West Nyack, N.Y.: Parker Publishing Company, 1970.

Educational Research Service. "Middle Schools in Action." Circular No. 2, 1969. Washington: National Education Association, March, 1969.

Educational Research Services, Inc. "Summary of Research on Middle Schools." Arlington, Virginia: Educational Research Services, 1976.

Eichhorn, Donald K. *The Middle School.* New York: Center for Applied Research in Education, 1966.

Frank, John, Jr. *Complete Guide to Co-Curricular Programs and Activities for the Middle Grades.* West Nyack, New York: Parker, 1976.

Gatewood, Thomas E. and Dilg, Charles A. *The Middle School We Need.* Washington: Association for Supervision and Curriculum Development, 1975.

George, Paul, ed. *The Middle School: A Look Ahead.* Fairborn, Ohio: National Middle School Association, 1977.

Grooms, M. Ann. *Perspective on the Middle School.* Columbus, Ohio: Charles E. Merrill, 1967.

Gruhn, William T. and Douglass, Harl R. *The Modern Junior High School.* 3d ed. New York: Ronald Press, 1971.

Hansen, John H. and Hearn, Arthur C. *The Middle School Program.* Chicago: Rand McNally, 1971.

Hertling, James E. and Getz, Howard G., eds. *Education for the Middle School Years: Readings.* Glenview, Illinois: Scott Foresman, 1971.

Howard, Alvin W. and Stoumbis, George C. *The Junior High and Middle School: Issues and Practices.* Scranton, Pa.: International Textbook Company, 1970.

Kagan, Jerome and Coles, Robert, eds. *Twelve to Sixteen: Early Adolescence.* New York: W. W. Norton and Co., Inc., 1972.

Kindred, Leslie W., ed. *The Intermediate Schools.* Englewood Cliffs, New Jersey: Prentice-Hall, 1968.

Kindred, Leslie W., et al. *The Middle School Curriculum: A Practitioner's Handbook.* Boston: Allyn and Bacon, 1976.

Leeper, Robert, ed. *Middle School in the Making.* "Readings from Educational Leadership." Washington: Association for Supervision and Curriculum Development, 1974.

Lipsitz, Joan. *Growing Up Forgotten: A Review of Research and Programs Concerning Early Adolescence.* Lexington, Massachusetts: D.C. Heath, 1977.

Lounsbury, John H. and Marani, Jean V. *The Junior High School We Saw: One Day in the Eighth Grade.* Washington: Association for Supervision and Curriculum Development, 1964.

McCarthy, Robert J. *The Ungraded Middle School.* West Nyack, New York: Parker, 1972.

Mitchell, John J. *Human Life: The Early Adolescent Years.* Toronto: Holt, Rinehart and Winston of Canada, 1974.

Moss, Theodore C. *Middle School.* Boston: Houghton Mifflin, 1969.

Murphy, Judith. *Middle Schools.* New York: Educational Facilities Laboratories, 1965.

Oliver, Albert I. *Curriculum Improvement.* 2d ed. New York: Harper & Row, 1977.

Overly, Donald E.; Kinghorn, John R.; and Preston, Richard L. *The Middle School: Humanizing Education for Youth.* Worthington, Ohio: Charles A. Jones, 1972.

Popper, Samuel H. *The American Middle School: An Organizational Analysis.* Waltham, Massachusetts: Blaisdell Publishers, 1967.

Pumerantz, Philip, and Galano, Ralph W. *Establishing Interdisciplinary Programs in the Middle School.* West Nyack, New York: Parker, 1972.

Schein, Bernard and Schein, Martha Pierce. *Open Classrooms in the Middle School.* West Nyack, New York: Parker, 1975.

Stoumbis, George C. and Howard, Alvin W., eds. *Schools for the Middle Years: Readings.* Scranton, Pennsylvania: International Textbook Company, 1969.

Stradley, William E. *A Practical Guide to the Middle School.* New York: The Center for Applied Research in Education, 1971.

Van Til, William; Vars, Gordon F.; and Lounsbury, John H. *Modern Education for the Junior High School Years.* 2d ed. Indianapolis: Bobbs-Merrill, 1967.

Vars, Gordon F., ed. *Common Learnings: Core and Interdisciplinary Team Approaches.* Scranton, Pa.: International Textbook Company, 1969.

———. *Guidelines for Junior High and Middle School Education.* Washington: National Association of Secondary School Principals, 1966.

Wiles, Jon. *Planning Guidelines for Middle School Education.* Dubuque, Iowa: Kendall/Hunt, 1976.

INDEX